PRODUCED BY THE PHILIP LIEF GROUP, INC.

Senior Writer:	Robert M. Utley
Writers:	Dale L. Walker, Jace Weaver, George R. Robinson, Shelley Rossell, Arnie Bernstein
Project Editors:	Claudia HCQ Sorsby, Jeannine Ciliotta
Editors:	Sona Vogel, Barbara Sullivan, Leslie T. Sharpe
Assistant Editors:	Naomi Starr, Jennifer Hirshlag
Copy Editors:	Joyce Nolan, Jack Roberts, Trumbull Rogers, Bruce Stevenson, Beth Wilson
Editorial Assistants:	Mary Kalamaras, Andrew Freiser
Additional Research:	Darren J. Talham
Production Manager:	Nina Neimark
Production Editor:	Kelli Daley
Designer:	Bernard Schleifer
Cartographer:	Arlene Goldberg
Composition:	NK Graphics

THE
AMERICAN
WEST

A MULTICULTURAL ENCYCLOPEDIA

Volume 1

ABILENE–BOUDINOT

GROLIER EDUCATIONAL CORPORATION

DANBURY, CONNECTICUT

Page i photos, clockwise from upper left: goldmining at Nome Beach, California; a Chinese family; cowboys; Arapaho Indians; Dawson, Yukon Territory; Calamity Jane. Center: Ben Pickett.

Published 1995 by Grolier Educational Corporation
Danbury, Connecticut 06816

Copyright © 1995 by The Philip Lief Group, Inc.

Published by arrangement with
The Philip Lief Group, Inc.
6 West 20th Street
New York, New York 10011

First Edition
ISBN: 0-7172-7421-7

Cataloging information to be obtained directly from
Grolier Educational Corporation.

Printed in the United States of America

CONTENTS: *Encyclopedia*

CONTENTS: *Volume 1*

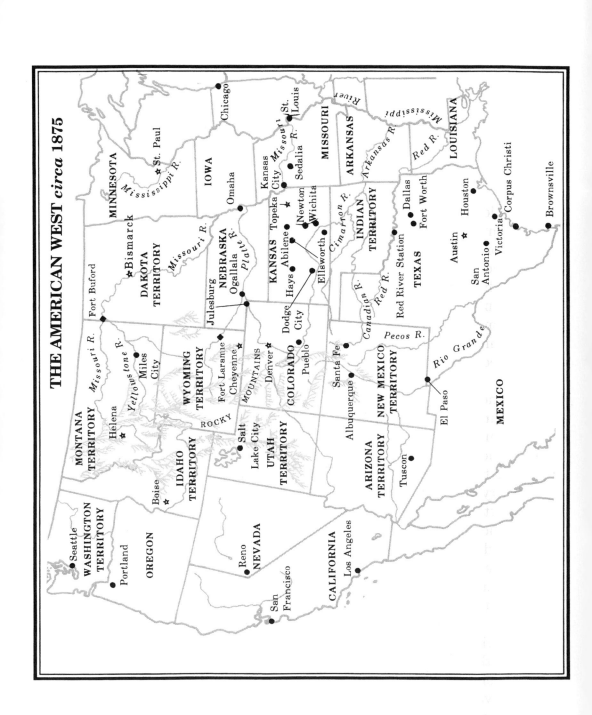

THE AMERICAN WEST *circa 1875*

ABOUT
The American West:
A Multicultural Encyclopedia

For many, the American West conjures up images of a wild, almost mythic place and time. During the nineteenth century, story after story was played out in the vast spaces of North America, from the Mississippi River to the Pacific Ocean. Many groups of Native Americans, each with its own rich cultural heritage, encountered waves of settlers and immigrants coming to the new land, bringing ideas and traditions of their own. It was a difficult, challenging time, in which Native Americans, explorers, settlers of all colors and creeds, miners, trappers, outlaws, and many others took part.

The American West: A Multicultural Encyclopedia takes a new look at this fascinating era. Designed in a straightforward, A–Z format, this ten-volume set will help students to learn about the varied and diverse groups of people who made up the West. Entries on Native American tribes, such as the Sioux and the Apaches, provide insight into their history and traditions, and record their perspective on the white settlers. Individuals such as Sequoyah, the Cherokee chief who was the first to create a written language for his people, and the legendary chief Sitting Bull are featured. Other entries describe the immigrants from Europe and China, who brought so many of their traditions to the New World, as well as the dangers and rewards they encountered.

Students will also find information on the major events of the century, including the Civil War, as well as the history of the states and cities, and the importance of geography in their development. The technology of the times, how such innovations as telegraphs and railroads transformed life, is also covered.

The American West has been designed to provide students with information in the most direct manner possible. The entries appear in alphabetical order, by last name, giving people, places, events, and concepts. To help the student find the connections between ideas and events, the books are completely cross-referenced; these references are marked in small capital letters. To maximize students' comprehension, a glossary of unfamiliar words and terms appears at the end of each volume. To make research as convenient and painless as possible, each volume contains a complete index for the whole set.

Perhaps most importantly, *The American West* enables students to put all this material into historical context. By providing a fresh, even-handed view of a much-mythologized period, *The American West* will help students to understand a unique and important part of their American history.

A

ABILENE, KANSAS

Abilene was the first of the great CATTLE TOWNS that sprang up after the CIVIL WAR as a transit point for shipping Texas cattle eastward. Until 1867 the village contained only a few log houses. But with the Kansas Pacific Railroad crossing at nearby Mud Creek and the CHISHOLM TRAIL connecting Abilene to TEXAS, the town was ripe for the cattle trade, and Kansas legislators realized its economic benefit. Because the hardy Texas longhorns carried a tick that caused the fatal Texas fever in other livestock, the state's legislators drew a quarantine line, allowing the cattle only on the western half of Kansas. Unfortunately, Abilene lay east of the line but Joseph Conroy, a wealthy livestock dealer who had purchased property around Abilene, fought and won approval to establish Abilene as a cattle shipping point. Over the next five years, nearly 3 million head of cattle were driven up the CHISHOLM TRAIL to Abilene, where they were fattened up and shipped east. The accompanying influx of COWBOYS and other transients brought quick wealth and wilder times, and saloons and brothels soon dotted the town. The famous JAMES BUTLER "WILD BILL" HICKOK worked as a law enforcement officer in Abilene until he was gunned down in DEADWOOD in Dakota Territory. But Abilene citizens and real estate dealers, who were tired of the corruption, joined the enraged farmers, who had lost acres of crops to the free-ranging cattle, to rally against the Abilene cattle market. These political battles caused the town to become more dependent on agri-

THE ABILENE CHRONICLE.

VOL. I. ABILENE, KANSAS, THURSDAY MORNING, MAY 12, 1870. NO. 9.

AN ORDINANCE

To Prevent Gambling.

Be it ordained by the Trustees of the town of Abilene,

SEC. 1. Every person who shall set up or keep any table or gambling device of any kind, adapted, devised, and designed for the purpose of playing any game of chance for money or property, and shall induce, entice, or permit any person to bet or play at or upon any such gaming table or gambling device, or on the side or against the keeper thereof, shall on conviction be fined in a sum not exceeding three hundred dollars nor less than twenty dollars, and imprisoned in the common jail of the town not exceeding thirty days.

SEC. 2. Every person who shall bet any money or property upon any gaming table, bank, or device prohibited by the foregoing section, or upon any game with cards, shall on conviction be fined in a sum not exceeding one hundred dollars nor less than ten dollars.

SEC. 3. Every person who shall permit any gaming table, bank, or device prohibited by section one of this ordinance, to be set up or used for the purpose of gaming in any house, building, shed, tent, booth, shelter, lot or premises to him belonging, or by him occupied, or of which he hath at the time possession or control, shall on conviction be fined not exceedidg five hundred dollars nor less than fifty dollars, or imprisoned in the common jail of the town not exceeding thirty days, or by both such fine and imprisonment.

SEC. 4. This ordinance shall take effect and be in force from and after the 20th of May 1870.

T. C. HENRY, Chairman.

Attest: G. L. BRINKMAN, Clerk,

AN ORDINANCE

Respecting Vagrancy

Be it ordained by. the Trustees of the town of Abilene,

SEC. 1. Any person who may be found loitering around houses of ill-fame, gambling houses, or places where liquors are sold or drank, without any legitimate means of support, or shall be the keeper or inmate of any house of ill-fame or gambling house, or engaged in any unlawful calling whatsoever, shall be deemed a vagrant, and upon conviction thereof may be fined in any sum not exceeding five hundred dollars, and unless such fine shall be paid the person so offending shall be committed to the common jail of the town, and shall work the same out on any public work of the town at the rate of two dollars per day for each day so committed.

SEC. 2. This ordinance shall take effect and be in force from and after May 20th 1870.

T. C. HENRY, Chairman.

Attest: G. L. BRINKMAN, Clerk.

AN ORDINANCE

To Regulate the sale of Spirituous Intoxicating Liquors.

Be it ordained by the Trustees of the town of Abilene,

SEC. 1. That before a license shall be granted to any person or persons applying for the same, to sell spirituous and intoxicating liquors within the incorporate limits of the town of Abilene, Kansas, or after the 20th day of May, 1870, any person so applying shall present to the Town Trustees a petition signed by a majority of the residents of the town of Abilene, of twenty-one years and over, both male and female, recommending said applicant as a suitable and safe person to vend the same, and requesting that a license be granted to him for such purpose.

SEC. 2. That upon every license granted as aforesaid, there shall be levied and collected a tax of one hundred dollars for the year, for the use and benefit of the town of Abilene, for every period of twelve months from and after the 20th day of May 1870.

SEC. 3. That all licenses granted under this ordinance shall terminate on the 20th of May 1871.

SEC. 4. That any person or persons, who, without procuring a license as herein aforesaid, shall sell or cause to be sold, any intoxicating liquors, shall, upon conviction, be fined any sum not less than five dollars nor more than forty dollars for each offense, and shall be imprisoned in the town jail until said fines and costs are paid.

SEC. 5. That before any person or persons be licensed to sell spirituous or intoxicating liquors under the provisions of this ordinance, they shall in their application state the name or names of the person or firm applying for the same, and shall state therein the house in which said liquors are to be sold. No transfer of said license from one party to another party, or from the place licensed to a different place shall be valid, unless application be first made to the Trustees of the town, and authority granted therefor.

SEC. 6. This ordinance to take effect from and after May 20, 1870.

T. C. HENRY, Chairman.

Attest: G. L. BRINKMAN, Clerk.

AN ORDINANCE

To Prohibit Drunkeness and Disorderly Conduct.

Be it ordaiued by the Trustees of the town of Abilene,

That any person found in a state of intoxication within the corporate limits of the town of Abilene, or any person guilty of noisy, riotous conduct, or threatening violence against any person or persons, or against the town of Abilene, or running horses on the public streets or alleys, or of lassoing any animal, or leading any wild animal with lasso, or lassoing any person or persons, or of discharging fire-arms within the town limits, shall on conviction thereof before the Court, be fined in any sum not less than five dollars nor more than twenty-five dollars for the first offense, and for the second offense not less than ten dollars nor more than fifty dollars, with costs of prosecution added in both first and second offense, and may be committed to the town jail for any length of time not exceeding five days, provided at the end of that time all costs and fines are paid.

This ordinance shall be in full effect and force from and after the 20th of May, 1870.

T. C. HENRY, Chairman.

Attest: G. L. BRINKMAN, Clerk.

AN ORDINANCE

Relating to the Carrying of Fire Arms and other Deadly Weapons.

Be it ordained by the Trustees of the town of Abilene,

SEC. 1. That any person who shall carry, within the limits of the town of Abilene, or commons, a pistol, revolver, gun, musket, dirk, bowie-knife, or other dangerous weapon upon his or their person or persons, either openly or concealed, except to bring the same and forthwith deposit it or them at their house, boarding house, store room or residence, shall be fined in a sum not less than ten dollars nor more than fifty dollars; and it shall be the duty of any town constable, or policeman of this town, to arrest and disarm any person violating this ordinance, and to deposit the arms so taken with the captain of the town police, to be by him kept until he is, by the magistrate taking cognizance of the offense of carrying arms as aforesaid, authorized to deliver the same to the person or persons from whom the same shall have been taken.

SEC. 2. Any and every person who shall be in violation of this ordinance, within the town of Abilene, or commons, and who shall refuse to deposit his or their arms with the constable or policeman as aforesaid, or shall resist any officer who may attempt to disarm him or them according to the provisions of section one of this obdinance, shall be imprisoned in the common gaol of the town not less than twenty-four hours nor more than ten days, and fined not less than $10 nor more than one hundred dollars: Provided, that the provisions of this ordinance shall not apply to the constable or any officer of the town of Abilene, while in the discharge of their duties as such constable or policeman.

SEC. 3. That any person who shall intentionally discharge any pistol, revolver or gun, within the town of Abilene, in any street, alley, highway, lot, house or other place where the life or limb of any person could be endangered, shall be punished by a fine not less than ten dollars nor more than one hundred dollars.

SEC. 4. This ordinance shall take effect and be in force from the 20th of May 1870.

T. C. HENRY, Chairman.

Attest: G. L. BRINKMAN, Clerk.

AN ORDINANCE

Relating to Houses of Ill-Fame.

Be it ordained by the Trustees of the town of Abilene.

SEC. 1. That any and every person or persons who shall keep or maintain, in this town, a house of ill-fame or prostitution, or a house in which disorderly, licentious, obscene, lewd, profane or indecent conduct or language is permitted or allowed, shall be fined not less than twenty-five dollars nor more than two hundred dollars, and the fact that such language occurring in said house shall be prima facie evidence that the same is permitted or allowed by the person who maintains or keeps such house.

SEC. 2. That any and every person who shall be an inmate or resident of a house of ill-fame or prostitution in this town, or who shall visit or frequent any such house for lewd, licentious, obscene or indecent purposes, shall, on conviction, be fined not less than ten dollars nor more than one hundred dollars, and the fact of any person being found in any such house in the night time, between the hours of eight o'clock, P. M., and five o'clock, a. m., shall be prima facie evidence of his or her frequenting the same for such purpose.

SEC. 3. That any and every person who shall attend, visit or frequent any place in the last preceeding section mentioned, and engage or take part in any of the acts, conduct or language therein specified, shall be fined not less than ten dollars nor more than one hundred dollars for each and every offense.

SEC. 4. That any person or persons who shall hereafter knowingly let, lease or rent any house, hall, tenement or other place in this town to any person or persons, for the purpose of keeping or maintaining therein any place as described in the preceeding sections of this ordinance, shall, on conviction, be punished by a fine not exceeding one hundred dollars, and not less than ten dollars for each day that he, she or they allow the same to be tenanted for such purpose or purposes, or who shall suffer the same to be used after any of the Constables of this town have given notice that the same has been declared a house of ill-fame.

SEC. 5. Be it ordained, that any person convicted for keeping a house of ill-fame, or being an inmate thereof, as provided in the foregoing sections, shall be removed by any of the town Constables without the corporate limits of this town, upon the order of the Court.

SEC. 6. This ordinance shall be in force from and after the 20th of May 1870.

T. C. HENRY, Chairman.

Attest: G. L. BRINKMAN, Clerk.

AN ORDINANCE

Relating to Sundry Offences.

Be it ordained by the Trustees of the town of Abilene:

SECTION 1. That any person found guilty of committing any of the several acts and offenses prohibited in this town, shall be subjected to the penalty herein provided for them respectively.

SEC. 2. That for distnrbing the peace of the town, or any lawful assembly of persons, or of any neighborhood, family, person or persons, or for indecent, obscene, improper or abusive language or conduct, or for any assault or affray, a fine of a sum not less than one nor more than one hundred dollars.

SEC. 3. For throwing stone or brick or pieces of wood or other hard substances in or across any building, street or alley of this town, or at or against any house, building, vehicle, person or animal, a fine shall be imposed of not less than one nor more than fifty dollars, at the discretion of the Court.

SEC. 4. For discharging any fire-arms, setting off fire crackers or squibs, throwing any fire balls or combustible substance, or making bonfires, within the limits of the town, a fine shall be imposed of not less than one nor more than twenty-five dollars: Provided, that this section shall not apply or be enforced on the first day of January, nor on the fourth day of July of each year: And provided further, that this provision may be applied to other days by the Trustees: Neither shall this section apply to the person authorized to keep a pistol gallery, nor to any gunsmith who may carefully discharge any fire-arms in the prosecution of his business, nor shall it apply to the person duly authorized to shoot dogs running at large in the town.

Attempts at law and order in Abilene brought revenue to the city but did little to stop crime and misconduct.

culture, and Texas ranchers began to look to Ellsworth, Kansas, as a place to conduct their profitable business.

ACOMAS

The Acomas, a tribe of PUEBLOS of the Keresan-language family, reside on and around Acoma Mesa, a 357-foot-high plateau about 60 miles west of Albuquerque, NEW MEXICO.

Though the Acomas' RESERVATION encompasses the

SMITHSONIAN INSTITUTE

This isolated mesa top location helped to protect the Acomas from their enemies.

towns of Acomita and McCartys, where most of the people live year-round, its emotional heart is the "Sky City" of Acoma (sometimes called Old Acoma), a traditional-style pueblo thought by many to be the oldest continuously inhabited site in the United States. Although the Keresan-speaking Pueblos entered the region later than some of their relatives, the Acomas are one of the few Pueblo tribes who were not forced to relocate as a result of interaction with the Spaniards.

The first European contact with Acomas was recorded by Fray Marcos de Niza in 1539. They were also visited briefly by FRANCISCO DE CORONADO's expedition in 1540. It was, however, the arrival of JUAN DE OÑATE in the area in 1598 that had the most lasting impact on the Acomas and other Pueblos. At the time of these early encounters, the Acomas, believed to number 5,000 to 10,000, ranged over approximately 5 million acres of territory.

Acoma pueblo, in western New Mexico, dates from approximately 1000 C.E.

Oñate came with 129 colonists who ultimately settled in SANTA FE. He sought to turn the Pueblos into a subject people, forcibly converting them to Catholicism and using them as involuntary labor. The Acomas also were taught to grow peaches, peppers, and wheat, and to raise sheep. The last of these skills became an important component of the Acoma economy into the twentieth century.

Along with other Pueblos, Acomas took part in the PUEBLO REVOLT OF 1680, which drove the Spaniards from the region. Enchanted Mesa, an important site for the Acomas, was fortified in 1694 by the Keresan-speaking Pueblos, who experienced hostility from other Pueblos following the return of the Spaniards because of their supposed allegiance to the foreigners.

Throughout the nineteenth century, the Acomas raised sheep. This practice, however, gradually gave way around the turn of the century to cattle ranching. Since the 1890s, the tribe has been unrelenting in its efforts to recover the lands that were taken from them. By 1900, their population had dwindled to an estimated 500; it since has recovered to around 4,000.

ADAMS-ONÍS TREATY
1819

This far-reaching treaty, negotiated by Secretary of State John Quincy Adams and Luis de Onís, Spanish minister in Washington, resulted in Spain's ceding the Floridas to the United States and in the establishment of the western boundary of the LOUISIANA PURCHASE.

Spain relinquished the Floridas (both the east and the west portions) because, with its colonial empire collapsing, it could neither promise to settlers protection from the Indians in the territory—a crisis solved temporarily by Andrew Jackson's Indian campaign in Florida in 1814—nor prevent the escape into Florida of American slaves. Moreover, as Adams pointed out, West Florida, on the Gulf of Mexico, was properly U.S. territory under the provisions of the Louisiana Purchase.

In exchange for the Floridas, and for all Spanish rights in the Oregon Territory, the United States agreed to nullify all damage claims by Americans against Spain and to assume payment of those claims up to the amount of $5 million.

Among the future ramifications of the Adams-Onís Treaty, none was to be more significant than the TEXAS question. Although Adams sought to include Texas among territories ceded to the United States in marking the southwestern boundary, he failed to win the support of the Monroe administration for this plan. The boundary was therefore established at the Sabine River, setting the stage for American-Mexican confrontations, revolution, and ultimate Texan independence in the coming three decades.

ADOBE

Adobe is a Spanish word (from the Arabic *at-tub,* the brick) meaning sun-dried bricks composed of a mix of clay and straw, the buildings made from those bricks, and the clay soil used in the making of these bricks. Moist adobe clay is very plastic and can easily be molded into almost any shape. Once it has dried, however, it is virtually indestructible. Indians recognized this characteristic at a very early date and used the muddy soil to make bowls, mugs, pitchers, and other vessels. They also used it in the construction of compact, multistory, apartment-like dwellings. The glint of the sun reflecting from those buildings later fueled the Span-

Pueblo homes made of adobe, the primary building material for these desert dwellers.

ish conquistadores' gold-hungry dreams of the Seven Cities of Cíbola.

Use of adobe came to the Southwest from MEXICO when the Pueblo people brought Mesoamerican culture with them. Later, the Spanish used the material to construct their own

Pueblo in New Mexico built of adobe bricks.

dwellings. Because adobe buildings are cheap, easy to build, and very energy efficient, from early days they were found as far north as Wyoming and Montana.

Because it was inexpensive, "adobe" was once synonymous with "inferior." For example, Mexican currency was once termed "dobe dollars." Today, however, it is identified with the SANTA FE style, and adobe houses can be found throughout the United States.

AFRICAN-AMERICANS IN THE WEST

The experience of black Americans in the West provides one of many examples of the complex dialectic of race in this nation's history. African-American history in the West is as fraught with contradiction and irony as any element in the story of the American West, an uneasy blend of triumph and tragedy side by side.

There were blacks in the West as early as there were whites. Black Estevan, one of the survivors of the ill-fated

An African-American cowboy, one of the many ethnically diverse men who went to work on the cattle ranches of the West.

African-American soldiers of Company B, 25th U.S. Infantry, outside their barracks at Fort Randall, Dakota Territory.

CABEZA DE VACA expedition, earned a reputation as a linguist and medicine man among the southwestern tribes during the early sixteenth century. The Coronado expedition included several black priests.

The tradition that these inclusions (perhaps unwittingly) established was continued in the eighteenth century and later. A list of the fur traders and trappers of the period features African-Americans in virtually every role. Jean Baptiste Point-du-Sable established a trading post at what is now Chicago. JIM BECKWOURTH was one of the most famous MOUNTAIN MEN. The LEWIS AND CLARK EXPEDITION included York, Clark's "manservant," who distinguished himself by his athletic feats, courage, and hunting ability. Jacob Dodson, a free black who was an integral part of JOHN C. FRÉMONT's second and third expeditions, became an experienced Indian fighter. Two of the Astorians, the trappers JOHN JACOB ASTOR sent to OREGON to establish his foothold there, were black.

However, as it did every other aspect of African-American life, SLAVERY affected all of the relationships between blacks and others on the frontier. Every frontier was a military one while the relations between settlers and Native Americans remained primarily hostile, and it was with great reluctance that white settlers allowed slaves to participate in the defense of settlements—Who would knowingly give a slave weapons?

In one case, in South Carolina during the Creek War of 1715, slaves were enlisted in the state militia. That was rare, and as their numbers grew, blacks were not allowed to repeat that experience. More typically, Spanish authorities in the Carolinas actively encouraged slaves to run away from their masters, and some tribes—notably the Creeks—gave shelter to runaways. In later years, these runaways acted as agents for Spain and France among the Creeks. Runaway slaves and freedmen often fought alongside both the Spanish and the SEMINOLES in Florida. Black Seminoles, the sons and daughters of runaway slaves, were at the heart of the 1835 Seminole War, which was as much a fight for black liberation as for red liberation.

Free blacks on the frontier during the same period may have enjoyed less discrimination than they would after emancipation. Communities were less settled, many formerly French-controlled regions still offered a fair degree of racial tolerance, and the freedmen were an integral part of the defense of the community. The black mountain men and fur traders were experienced fighters who knew the conditions of the regions they frequented and often functioned as interpreters or guides.

In other areas, a free African-American might be the only skilled craftsman. In one Virginia community, near Staunton, the blacksmith and the farrier were both freedmen. Other freedmen of the antebellum period chose to follow the westward expansion; Texas under the Mexican Republic was particularly attractive because of its comparative racial tolerance.

The CALIFORNIA GOLD RUSH affected African-Americans as much as it did everyone else who heard of the discovery at SUTTER'S MILL. Until that time, California's black population had been a small one, composed mainly of deserting sailors. This latter group swelled the ranks of the Forty-niners; both blacks and whites jumped ship at the chance of striking it rich. In addition, many southern prospectors brought their slaves with them, and many freedmen and runaways sought work as miners or in the businesses that sprang up around the goldfields. By the 1850 census, there were nearly 1,000 blacks in California, concentrated primarily in Sacramento and San Francisco. (In Colorado blacks were barred from filing mining claims, which forced runaway slave Barney Ford to find a different line of work in Denver during the 1860s; he ended up as a successful restaurateur and hotel owner.)

California was a free state. Nevertheless, black Californians were denied the right to vote and to an education, and were consistently discriminated against in the court system, where they were prohibited from testifying against whites. The response to these injustices, the California Colored Convention, may rightly be called one of the first black civil rights organizations in the West, if not the entire United States. The group collected thousands of signatures on petitions opposing the discriminatory court system, but the Democratic state legislature chose to ignore them.

It is one of the nastier ironies of American history that

A racially mixed group of cowboys.

Oklahoma had a sizable black population before it had a white one, because each of the FIVE CIVILIZED TRIBES, formally inaugurated in 1859 in Oklahoma, included slave owners. These Native Americans were split by the coming of the CIVIL WAR, with the Chickasaws, Choctaws, and Seminoles siding with the Confederacy and the Cherokees and Creeks (see FIVE CIVILIZED TRIBES) with the Union. Nevertheless, the Confederacy negotiated treaties with all five. Needless to say, the black members of the tribes were unanimous in their support of the Union. However, military action in the territories resulted in suffering for all.

Black troops fought in the Civil War, particularly in the western theater. Black and Indian regiments fought in Kansas and in the Indian Territory in campaigns marked by a high level of brutality; Confederate guerrillas disdained to take black prisoners. From these units came the men who would become the legends of the black West: seasoned Indian fighters like Charley Tyler and Britton Johnson, and the black units of the regular army, the BUFFALO SOLDIERS.

Many frontier army posts were staffed almost entirely with black troops (under white officers). They fought against hostile Native Americans and Mexican border raiders alike. The campaigns against the APACHE chiefs VICTORIO and Nana were conducted primarily by black troops. In the 20 years of the fiercest INDIAN WARS (1870–1890), 14 African-Americans won the Congressional Medal of Honor.

At the same time, black COWBOYS were becoming a common sight along the cattle trails. Ranch cooks frequently were African-Americans, and many blacks were skilled horse breakers as well; black rodeo and Wild West Show stars like BILL PICKETT were numerous. Black lawmen could be found, too; one of "Hanging Judge" ISAAC PARKER'S most effective deputies was Bass Reeves, who served as a federal marshal for 35 years.

As the HOMESTEAD ACT attracted would-be farmers to the West, many former slaves swelled their numbers. Perhaps the most famous of these were the EXODUSTERS, who migrated to Kansas in the late 1870s; others pushed on to Oklahoma and Colorado.

Within the still independent Indian nations, in Oklahoma and the Indian Territory, blacks probably enjoyed greater social, economic, and political equality than elsewhere in the United States, perhaps in some part because of their hostility to the encroaching whites. When political struggles broke out between full-blood and mixed-blood Native Americans, the blacks tended to side with the full-bloods. Not surprisingly, when Oklahoma was admitted to the Union in 1907, racial discrimination against both blacks and Indians became the law and practice once more. In fact, one of the last outbursts of Native American armed resistance to white oppression, the Crazy Snake rebellion in March 1909—an attempt to regain Indian independence in the state—drew most of its support from black Creeks and Seminoles.

Although Jim Crow laws, with their enforced segregation, were for the most part a southern phenomenon, de facto segregation existed throughout the West in the post-Reconstruction era. The National Association for the Advancement of Colored People (NAACP) found the West a fertile region for organizing; it had six chapters in the region by 1914, after only five years of existence. One of the organization's first legal victories occurred in Oklahoma, when the U.S. Supreme Court ruled in 1915 that the state's "grandfather clause" was racially discriminatory and therefore unconstitutional.

ALAMO, BATTLE OF THE
1836

In 1803, the LOUISIANA PURCHASE placed the southwestern border of the United States contiguous to that of Spanish-ruled TEXAS. After MEXICO had gained independence from Spain in 1821, its government encouraged the emigration to Texas of U.S. citizens willing to renounce their citizenship. By 1836, some 30,000 Americans had settled in what was then the northern Mexican state of Coahuila y Texas.

In 1834, General Antonio López de Santa Anna took control of the Mexican government, abolished the 1824 constitution, and declared martial law. In January 1836 he gathered an army at Saltillo, 200 miles south of the RIO GRANDE, and marched north to extinguish the growing rebellion among the Texans.

At this time, just a month before the Texas declaration of independence from Mexico, the Alamo mission in San Antonio had been converted into a fortress. It was built in the form of a large rectangle with a smaller one attached to the eastern side. The church and a powder magazine occupied the southeastern corner of the three-acre bastion, the whole of which was protected by earthen walls that averaged 12 feet high. Wooden parapets to support gun batteries had been constructed, and irrigation ditches around the outside perimeter of the improvised fortress added to the difficulty of access. ADOBE and wood barracks for officers and men were located around three walls of the large rectangle, and a

An 1879 drawing showing President-General Antonio Lopez de Santa Anna and his troops storming the Alamo.

makeshift hospital, a cattle pen, and a horse corral along the walls of the smaller one, adjacent to the church.

The Alamo had been founded in 1718 as the Misión de San Antonio de Valero (named for the Marquis of Valero, a Spanish viceroy in Mexico). The original mission of adobe huts and church had been moved several times to various sites along the San Antonio River. Its chief function was to convert the Xarames, Pampoa, Payaya, and Sana tribes of the area. The mission received its popular name about 1801 when Spanish troops from the pueblo of San José y Santiago del Alamo del Parras were stationed there (alamo is Spanish for a type of tree).

There is some evidence that if SAM HOUSTON, commander in chief of the Texas Army, had had his way, the Alamo would never have been defended. Adamantly opposed to fighting behind fortifications, he sought a battle in the open, on familiar terrain, where cavalry and mobile infantry could extend the Mexican lines and distance them from their supplies. Houston may have ordered the removal of the Alamo's guns (one 18-pounder and perhaps 20 smaller, twelve-, eight-, six-, and four-pound cannon), the destruction of the Alamo walls, and evacuation of the site.

Houston is believed to have sent these orders with his old friend Colonel JAMES BOWIE, a 40-year-old, Kentucky-born rowdy who had married into a prominent San Antonio family. Bowie was ill—perhaps with tuberculosis—and if he had such orders, seems not to have taken them seriously. At the Alamo, where he found the garrison eager to fight, he assisted in shoring up the gun emplacements and injured himself while helping hoist a cannon onto the ramparts. He was ill and in bed during the siege, so command of the garrison fell to William Barret Travis, aged 27, a South Carolina–born lawyer by training and a soldier by choice.

On February 16, when Santa Anna, with about 2,000 men, 21 cannon, 1,800 pack mules, and some 250 wagons and carts of ammunition and supplies, crossed the Rio Grande, Travis's Alamo command consisted of about 150 men. Included in the number were a dozen Tennessee Mounted Volunteers led by the legendary marksman, backwoods orator, and three-time congressman, DAVID CROCKETT. Travis had 17 serviceable medium-to-small cannon plus the 18-pounder located on the southwest corner of the fort. Ammunition included standard balls and backup loads of loose horseshoe scrap, nails, and stones. The artillery was commanded by a Tennessee blacksmith, Captain Almeron Dickinson.

Santa Anna, with two brigades of infantry and one of cavalry, plus artillery units and *zapadores* (sappers)—a force numbering perhaps 4,000 (estimates vary)—began the siege of the Alamo on February 24, hammering the walls with the light field artillery and heavy siege guns he had brought from Saltillo.

Hoping for reinforcements, Travis sent a courier to Colonel James Fannin in Goliad, about 90 miles away. Fannin set out on February 26 with over 300 men, but his supply train broke down, and various other mishaps caused him to abandon the march and return to Goliad. Travis's only reinforcements came on March 1, when 32 volunteers from Gonzales arrived, raising the Alamo force to about 183 fighting men.

On the second day of the siege, Travis sent through the Mexican lines his famous "To the People of Texas and all Americans in the world" message, an appeal that, although issued too late to assist him, would soon be heard around the world. It contained the news that the Alamo was besieged by SANTA ANNA's forces and ended with the pronouncement "I shall never surrender or retreat . . . I call on you, in the name of liberty, of patriotism, and of everything dear to American character, to come to our aid with all dispatch." The last three words—*"Victory or Death!"*—were underlined three times.

On March 5, the tenth day, Travis told his defenders there would be no relief or reinforcements and that the options were to surrender, to try to escape through the Mexican lines, or to stand and fight. Crockett said he didn't like being "hemmed up" and preferred to "march out and die in the open air." Only one man elected to escape, however; he made his way over the wall to safety that night.

At 5 o'clock on the morning of March 6, 1836, Santa Anna began his assault, sending four columns of some 500 men each against the four walls of the Alamo. The trail-toughened Mexican infantry moved forward with scaling ladders, axes, pikes, picks, and muskets with bayonets. Behind them, bugles blared a degüello—a dirge signifying death to all the enemy—and as they closed on the Alamo walls, they shouted, *"Viva Santa Anna!"*

The battle quickly became a melee. On the north wall, Travis, sword in hand, shouted encouragement to his cannoneers; Crockett and his Tennesseans on the south wall fought off the attackers on their scaling ladders in desperate

Susanna Dickinson one of the only survivors of the Battle at the Alamo.

The only U.S. flag to survive the Alamo, from a Louisiana company.

hand-to-hand clubbing, hacking, and bayoneting; the Mexican columns on the east and west veered off and joined a battering ram force on the north side. The dense clot of men at the foot of that wall came under withering fire from above. There were two great assaults, a momentary lull, then the furious fighting resumed as Santa Anna ordered up his reserves and struck the north wall again. There Travis, firing his shotgun into the massed infantry below, was struck in the head by a musket ball and tumbled, dead, down the cannon ramp. Meantime, on the south wall a six-pound cannon in a lunette that jutted out from the wall, and the great 18-pounder on the southwest corner, did great damage to the attackers.

But the end was near: on the northeastern wall, a Mexican officer and his men made their way through a breach and into the Alamo's plaza. On the west side, the thinning ranks of defenders could not prevent the enemy from spilling over the parapets. Santa Anna's force poured in unchecked, and the fighting became a savage hand-to-hand, backs-to-the-wall combat. Near the front of the church and hospital, Crockett and his Tennesseans were caught in the open and all killed; on the roof of the church, James Butler Bonham, a boyhood friend of Travis's, and some artillerymen tried to fire their cannon on the plaza below and inflicted some severe if momentary damage before being picked off by Mexican musket fire.

Santa Anna's troops, following the order that there would be no quarter and no prisoners, entered each room of the hospital and barracks, killing all inside. Forty defenders were killed in the hospital. From his cot in a barracks room on the south wall, Bowie is said to have used the two pistols given him by Crockett, then rose to defend himself with his famous knife before being bayoneted to death. One of his sisters-in-law, who was present, later said the Mexican soldiers "tossed his body on their bayonets until their uniforms were dyed with his blood." In the powder magazine on the north side of the church, the Irish-born ordnance chief, Robert Evans, tried to light a trail of gunpowder to blow up the magazine and the church. He was killed before he could do so.

The Alamo fell at 6:30 A.M.; the battle had lasted 90 minutes.

Five defenders survived long enough to be brought before Santa Anna. He was furious at seeing them and ordered them shot. Now all the defenders were dead.

Ten Mexican women (among them two of Bowie's sisters-in-law, who had witnessed his death) and children survived. The others inside who lived to tell the story were Susanna Dickinson, wife of the artillery commander; her 15-month-old daughter, Angelina; and Travis's slave, a man known only as Joe.

The bodies of the defenders were placed between layers of wood and set afire; trenches were dug for the Mexican dead. Santa Anna's casualties are believed to have been at least 600, and of that number at least 200 were dead.

The Alamo victory proved costly for Santa Anna. "Remember the Alamo!" became the rallying cry as the Mexicans were driven from Texas the following April 21 when, at SAN JACINTO, Sam Houston and 800 men met and defeated Santa Anna's 3,000-man army, capturing the general and forcing him to sign a peace treaty that recognized Texas's independence.

ALASKA

Following its disastrous defeat in the Crimean War (1854–1856), Russia, desperate to pay off its war debts, authorized its minister in Washington, Edouard de Stoeckl, to sound out U.S. interest in purchasing Russian America— Alaska. (England, which had defeated Russia in the Crimean War and which Russia feared might seize Alaska, was not interested in acquiring that vast terra incognita.)

Stoeckl's initial talks in Washington were interrupted by the Civil War, but in 1867 he was instructed to renew efforts to sell the territory to the Americans. The discussions began in March 1867 between Stoeckl and Secretary of State William H. Seward, one of the nation's greatest expansionists. Seward was anxious to get the Russian territory and, without authorization, offered Stoeckl $5.5 million. When

LIBRARY OF CONGRESS

Residents of Deering Alaska, congregate around the local shops in 1903.

PROVINCIAL ARCHIVES, VICTORIA

The lavishly decorated house of a chilkat chief in Alaska.

Stoeckl contacted St. Petersburg, saying he would ask for a higher price, Seward, with the president's support, presented the issue at a cabinet meeting, requesting authorization to spend up to $7 million to purchase the territory. On March 23, Seward met with Stoeckl again, and the main points of the sale were agreed upon: the United States would pay $7.2 million for Russian America. After a tough congressional battle, the purchase was ratified and the American flag was raised on October 18, 1867, over Sitka, capital of Russian America for 68 years.

Seward in later years considered the acquisition of Alaska as his greatest accomplishment. He estimated it would take a generation before the American people would understand its importance. Actually, it would take 30 years before the American people, or their representatives in Wash-

Tlingits dressed up for a pot latch in Sitka, Alaska.

ington, would pay much attention to the vast possession to the north (which was called in newspaper editorials and among his colleagues in Washington "Seward's Folly" and "Seward's Icebox").

The United States had purchased 586,400 square miles of new territory, a piece of land twice the size of Texas (indeed, one-fifth the size of the entire United States) bounded by the Arctic and Pacific oceans, the Canadian Yukon to the east and Russian Siberia, 55 miles across the Bering Strait, to the West. The new acquisition, it was soon learned, contained over 15,000 square miles of waterways, the highest mountain in North America (subsequently named Mount McKinley), and seemingly boundless resources of minerals, furs, fish, and timber.

At the time it was acquired, Alaska had about 30,000 indigenous Indians and fewer than 1,000 other inhabitants, mostly Russian and American trappers concentrated around

Sitka, the town on Baranov Island (founded in 1799) that remained the capital of the territory until 1900. Some attention was paid to Alaska in 1880 when gold was discovered in the Alaskan Panhandle by Joseph Juneau. Other gold strikes in the region—in the Yukon Territory in 1896 and at the sites of Nome (1898) and Fairbanks (1902)—brought attention to the territory by the end of the century.

In 1884 the territory became a civil district with a governor, and the former goldrush town of Juneau became the capital in 1900. It was not until 1906 that Alaska sent a territorial delegate to Congress. Alaska became the forty-ninth state in 1959.

ALDER GULCH

Site of the gold strike in southwest MONTANA in 1863, the Alder Gulch placer deposits were discovered by prospector William H. "Bill" Fairweather, a Canadian who came to Montana in 1862. He and a group of goldseekers spent the winter of 1862 at Bannack, 65 miles to the east of Alder Gulch, and intended to join an expedition the next spring to prospect along the Yellowstone River. After a brief period in which he and his partners were taken captive by CROW Indians, Fairweather found the first nugget on Alder Creek on May 26, 1863.

The placer gold along the creekbed turned out to be significantly rich and by June 1863, a mining district was formed. (The Alder Gulch mining camp was named Varina in honor of the wife of Jefferson Davis, president of the Confederacy, but was soon changed to VIRGINIA CITY.)

Within eight months there were several hundred buildings along the creek and gulch and within a year, Virginia City's population was 4,000. It is estimated that $10 million in gold was taken from the Alder Gulch claims in 1863 and

William Fairweather, one of the first to find gold in Alder Gulch.

$30 million in the first three years. Virginia City was incorporated in 1864 and became Montana's territorial capital, a distinction it enjoyed until 1876.

Alder Gulch miners were chief among those terrorized and murdered by nightriders and claim jumpers during the first two years of the strike. This situation resulted in the formation of a vigilance committee which brought the outlaws to justice. Twenty-one of the culprits were hanged in January 1864, including their leader, HENRY PLUMMER, sheriff of Bannack and Virginia City.

By 1870 the Alder Gulch placers had played out. Virginia City, like TOMBSTONE, Arizona Territory, hung on and is today a tourist town with a tiny permanent population and a historical museum depicting its boom days. Bill Fairweather, who found the first gold in the gulch, squandered his riches in drunken sprees, prospected briefly in ALASKA, and returned to Montana, where he died on August 25, 1875.

ALEUTS

There has been considerable confusion concerning the origin and identity of the Aleuts. The origin of the word is unknown but probably derives from their word *aliat,* meaning "island." Logically, the Unangan-speaking inhabitants of

An Aleutian seal hunt.

the Aleutian archipelago call themselves Aleut, but so do their traditional enemies, the Sugpiaq of the Kodiak archipelago and Prince William Sound, as well as some Yup'ik Eskimos. Anthropologists and linguists, however, generally consider the Unangans to be Aleut.

The Aleuts lived by hunting, primarily seals but also caribou, walruses, and whales. As was true of the bison on the Plains, these animals provided almost everything necessary for daily life. Every part of the animal was used for food or for shelter, clothing, tools—even sleds and boats.

The Aleuts were the first in the New World to encounter Russians, beginning with Vitus Bering in 1741. They were often killed by Russian hunters, and in the eighteenth and nineteenth centuries were forced to work for the Russian-American Company. Many were deported and resettled on the Pribilof Islands, on the Kurile Islands north of Japan, in CALIFORNIA, and at Russian outposts throughout ALASKA. These factors, plus disease (including frequent outbreaks of smallpox), reduced the Aleut population of 25,000 at the time of Russian contact to around 2,000 by the time the United

States acquired Alaska in 1867. The Russian Orthodox Church remains an important force in Aleut culture.

The name Alaska derives from an Aleut term meaning "Great Land," their term for the mainland.

LIBRARY OF CONGRESS

Clay Allison in bandages after accidentally shooting himself in the leg.

ALLISON, ROBERT CLAY
1841–1887

Born in Tennessee, Allison served the Confederacy during the CIVIL WAR, including as a scout for Nathan Bedford Forrest and as a spy. He made his way to Texas after the surrender at Appomattox, and during trail drives from Texas to Kansas, and stints as a cowboy in New Mexico and Colorado, earned his reputation as a gunman and a magnet for trouble.

Some of Allison's exploits are probably apocryphal. He is said to have killed a man in a knife duel over an open grave; another story has him taking revenge on a dentist who pulled the wrong tooth by pulling one of the dentist's teeth at gunpoint; another has him forcing DODGE CITY lawman BAT MASTERSON to back down from a gunfight.

In fact, Allison was a drunk and a psychotic killer. His first reported killing occurred in 1874, when he shot a man near the Canadian River in New Mexico, and there is ample evidence that he was involved in other killings during the 1870s in Texas, New Mexico, Colorado, and Kansas. He died on July 3, 1887, when he fell from a freight wagon and a wheel rolled over his head. He is buried in Pecos, Texas.

AMERICAN FUR COMPANY

This company, which in its 56-year history became the most powerful of all North American fur enterprises, was founded in April 1808 by JOHN JACOB ASTOR, a German-born entrepreneur who had come to America in 1793.

The American Fur Company, the parent enterprise under which Astor launched such subsidiaries as the Pacific Fur Company and the South West Company (covering the Great Lakes region), had by 1822 become a formidable force in the fur trade. That year Astor opened a Western Department in ST. LOUIS for the MISSOURI RIVER trade, and in 1827 he acquired the Columbia Fur Company, combining it with the AFC to form what was called the Upper Missouri Outfit. In 1828 he established a trading post, FORT UNION, at the confluence of the Yellowstone and Missouri rivers.

In the 1830s, Astor, who had previously concentrated on the Upper Missouri and Pacific Northwest trade, moved into the ROCKY MOUNTAINS. There his chief rival was the ROCKY MOUNTAIN FUR COMPANY, created in 1826. By 1834, Astor had absorbed the remnants of Rocky Mountain Fur, but with the trade in decline, sold his fur interests that year and retired to manage real estate and other interests in New York City. In 1864, the American Fur Company was sold to the Northwest Fur Company.

The key to the AFC's success was Astor's enormous wealth and political influence. Despite losing ASTORIA, his base of operations at the mouth of the COLUMBIA RIVER in Oregon Territory, during the War of 1812, he manipulated federal laws to abolish government-owned factories and to exclude any but U.S. citizens from engaging in fur trade management and ownership. At its peak of operation, the AFC controlled three-quarters of the American fur trade. (See also FUR TRADE.)

ANASAZI CULTURE

Anasazi is a NAVAJO name given to the cliff-dwelling culture of the Southwest. The name is generally translated as "ancient people," but it may also mean "enemy ancestors."

The Anasazis flourished in the Four Corners area from about 600 until 1300. Their culture, architecture, and pottery styles strongly reflect Mesoamerican influence. They began as wandering bands of hunters but for unknown reasons developed a more sedentary lifestyle as corn farmers. At first they lived in pit houses dug out of the earth and covered with a superstructure of wood and mud; over the centuries their dwellings evolved into more traditional pueblo styles.

Anasazi culture reached its zenith beginning around 900. During this period, great cliff dwellings up to five stories tall were constructed at Chaco Canyon, Canyon de Chelly, MESA VERDE, and Tsegi Canyon, as well as elsewhere. The reasons for this shift are unknown. It has generally been assumed that the Anasazis moved into these high, inaccessible sites to seek protection from enemies. Others, however, have suggested that it may have had a religious purpose—perhaps the people sought to live closer to the sky.

Around 1200 the Anasazi began to abandon their cliff dwellings throughout COLORADO, ARIZONA, and NEW MEXICO. As with much about the Anasazis, the reasons for this action are mysterious. Drought, soil erosion leading to crop failure, disease, warfare, and religious decree have all been sug-

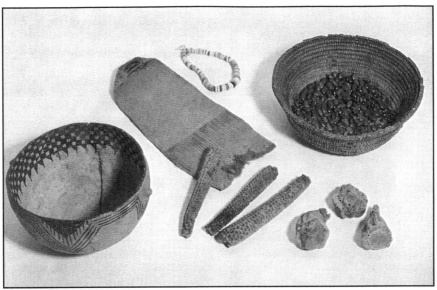

Remains of the Anasazis from about 700 C.E. Shown, clockwise from left, are a pottery bowl based on a basketry design, a yucca fiber sandal, a bead bracelet, a basket of beans, and squash and corn.

gested. Perhaps it was some combination of many of these factors. At any rate, by 1300 the Anasazis had left the cliff dwellings completely. It also is unknown whether the Navajo, who were moving into the area around this time, had anything to do with the abandonment. Shortly after the Anasazi cities were evacuated, however, they were occupied by Navajos.

For many years it was thought that the Anasazis disappeared completely. More recent evidence suggests otherwise. Archaeology reveals no great cultural shift in the area. Also, during this period surrounding towns experienced significant population increases and new villages sprang up. It now appears that following their departure from their cliff dwellings, the Anasazis joined related communities. They thus became the ancestors of modern-day PUEBLO INDIANS.

ANTI-CHINESE RIOTS IN THE WEST

During this series of violent uprisings, Chinese immigrants were attacked by workers who feared losing their jobs to the foreign-born laborers.

Chinese workers (also known as "coolies") were often hired because of their willingness to work long hours for low wages. Consequently, they became a prized source of cheap human labor for employers. Because the Chinese were of a different racial and cultural background, they were subject to many prejudices and misunderstandings on the part of whites.

Resentment grew toward the Chinese among white workers, who feared these foreigners were taking their jobs. Employers considered the Chinese "docile" and easily bossed, a situation largely due to language difficulties. The Chinese workers would not complain about poor job conditions, which enabled bosses to exploit white workers as well. During the late 1860s, anti-coolie associations were organized in CALIFORNIA and led random attacks on Chinese workers. There were also suspicious fires at factories employing Chinese workers.

By the 1870s this violence had escalated. Although the Chinese were only 8 percent of California's population during the 1870s, they constituted about one-quarter of the work force. Bolstered by Denis Kearney's Workingmen's Party, anti-Chinese riots spread throughout the West, reaching their height in the mid-1880s.

In 1871, two Chinese groups battled in Los Angeles. This infighting led to street violence, resulting in the death of a prominent white Los Angeles resident. An angry mob stormed a building housing many Chinese, and lynched eight residents. Chinese homes were looted by rioters. When the riot finally ended, 19 Chinese workers had been killed.

In September 1885, the UNION PACIFIC RAILROAD decided to replace white workers in Rock Springs, Wyoming, coal

Anti-Chinese riot.

mines with cheaper Chinese laborers. Anti-Chinese violence broke out. Almost 30 of the foreign-born workers were killed in the ensuing riot, and 15 were injured. Wyoming's governor called on President Grover Cleveland to send in federal troops to restore order to the area.

Other riots erupted throughout the West while laborers continued to blame the Chinese for deteriorating work environments and low pay. Vigilante mobs forced Chinese residents to leave towns in California and Washington. President Cleveland sent more troops west in 1886, this time to Seattle, Washington, where anti-Chinese riots had boiled over and some 400 Chinese residents were driven from their homes by enraged whites. Fearing for their lives, Chinese workers and their families scattered, some fleeing to the large Chinese community in San Francisco. All the racial violence eventually led to the passage of the CHINESE EXCLUSION ACT. (See also CHINESE IN THE WEST.)

MUSEUM OF NEW MEXICO

Juan Bautista de Anza.

ANZA, JUAN BAUTISTA DE
1735–1788

The son and grandson of soldiers serving in northern New Spain, Juan Bautista de Anza, whose father was killed by the APACHES in 1739, was born in Fronteras, Sonora, Mexico. He volunteered for military service at age 17. During the first 20 years of his military career, he established himself as an indefatigable Apache fighter in the Gila River area of modern-day Arizona, rising to captain and commander of the presidio at Tubac.

In January 1774, Anza, commanding a force of 34 men, set out to blaze a trail from Sonora to Alta California. The expedition established the presidio of San Gabriel, north of modern Los Angeles, and pushed on to Monterey, arriving there in April. Upon returning to Sonora, Anza was promoted to lieutenant colonel; the viceroy in Mexico City later sent him back to California with a party of 240 colonizers and soldiers. After a six-month march, Anza and his force reached the great bay named for St. Francis of Assisi, and in March 1776, founded the presidio of SAN FRANCISCO.

After a brief period as commander of the Sonoran garrisons, Anza was named governor of NEW MEXICO and arrived in SANTA FE in December 1778. His prowess as an Indian fighter was quickly tested, for the isolated provincial capital lay in the epicenter of raids by APACHES, UTES, NAVAJOS, and COMANCHES. Together with his efforts to reduce the number of missions and consolidate those remaining to make them easier to defend, Anza's focus in 1779 was to strengthen Santa Fe's defenses and to campaign against the Comanches and their chief, Cuerno Verde ("Green Horn," from the single green-painted buffalo horn the Comanche leader wore as part of his headdress). In a dispatch to his superiors in Mexico City, Anza characterized Cuerno Verde as the "scourge of the kingdom." He set out in August 1779 for the Upper Rio Grande to deal with the redoubtable chief and his band.

With a force that eventually swelled to 600 men, made up of soldiers, settlers, and 160 PUEBLO and UTE volunteers, Anza trailed the Comanches to a camp in a valley east of the Continental Divide in Colorado, near the Sierra de Almagre (later named Pike's Peak). He defeated them decisively and deployed his forces to await the return of Cuerno Verde and his band from a raid on Taos. The Taos presidio, thanks to Anza's work, had been well fortified, so its garrison successfully repelled the Comanche attack. On September 3, 1779, Anza's huge force and Cuerno Verde's 50-odd Comanches clashed in battle. Anza later described the famous chief riding forward, "his spirit proud and superior to all his followers," and said with finality: "I determined to have his life, and his pride and arrogance precipitated him to this end." The battle resulted in the death of Cuerno Verde, his son, four other chiefs, and ten other Comanches. One man in Anza's force was wounded.

By 1786, through Anza's efforts, the Spanish had established peace with the Comanches, Utes, Navajos, and HOPIS. In 1788, Anza returned to Sonora, where he served briefly as commander of the presidio of Tucson. He died on December 19, 1788, and was buried at Arizpe, in the church of Nuestra Señora de la Asunción.

APACHES

The Apaches are an ATHAPASKAN tribe of Indians residing mainly in NEW MEXICO and ARIZONA. The name, derived from the Zuni word for "enemy," was originally applied by that tribe to the NAVAJOS (to whom the Apache are closely related). The principal divisions of the Apaches are the Chiricahua, Mescalero, Mimbreno (eastern Chiricahua), Lipan, and Jicarilla.

Before 1000, the Apaches lived on the Plains, where some continued to live as late as 1700. The horse and the introduction of firearms, however, allowed the COMANCHES and UTES to push them into the Southwest. They probably began arriving in the area around 1400. Thereafter, they defended a large territory against all arrivals.

Pressure from the Apaches helped weaken the Spanish

and contributed to the success of the PUEBLO REVOLT OF 1680. From 1685 until 1786, the tribe waged constant war against the Spanish, inhibiting their occupation of the region. The Spanish responded with a variety of stratagems—mostly unsuccessful—to control the Indians, including a bounty for scalps of Apache dead.

After the Spaniards, the Apaches fought the Mexicans. When the United States annexed the region following the MEXICAN WAR, it regarded the tribe as a conquered people. The Apaches considered themselves joint victors in a common war with Mexico. The tribe now fought both Mexicans and Americans.

When the U.S. Army occupied New Mexico in 1862, General JAMES CARLETON was determined to keep Union supply lines, which ran through Apache territory, open. He planned to do so by eliminating the Apaches. The Apache leader, MANGAS COLORADAS, and his son-in-law, COCHISE, fought back. Mangas was captured and murdered. A number of Apaches were defeated and sent to a RESERVATION at Bosque Redondo.

LIBRARY OF CONGRESS

Apache women gathering firewood on the reservation.

An Apache warrior.

An Apache chief.

Army scouts on the reservation shared by Kiowas and Comanches seek a site for a military post.

Following the war's end and Carleton's departure, the United States sought to confine all the Apaches to reservations. The Apaches' fame rests largely on their resistance to this policy. From 1866 until 1886 a series of Apache leaders (Cochise, VICTORIO, Juh, Nana, GERONIMO) and their followers fought the federal forces to a virtual standstill. It took 5,000 troops to force the surrender of Geronimo and his band of just 36, in 1886, to end the Apache Wars.

Nalin, an Apache girl.

Kiowa chief Little Mountain, painted by George Catlin in 1834.

Kiowa chief Lone Wolf.

Geronimo and his followers were imprisoned at Fort Marion, Florida. Later they were moved to Fort Sill, Indian Territory. Geronimo died at Fort Sill in 1909.

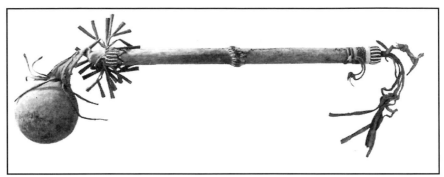

A stone-headed Apache war club.

ARAPAHOS

The Arapahos are an Algonquian tribe of Indians, traditionally closely associated with the CHEYENNES.

Arapaho tradition says that they were originally a farming people from around the Red River Valley in northern MINNESOTA. Probably sometime between 1675 and 1700, forced out by the CHIPPEWAS and SIOUX, they moved onto the Plains and became mounted buffalo hunters. Shortly thereafter, they split. The GROS VENTRE (or Atsina) moved northwest into Canada. The Arapahos moved southwest, and formed a close alliance with the Cheyennes. After continual warfare with the Sioux, CROWS, and other tribes, they migrated southwest, splitting again. The Northern Arapahos settled near the North Platte River in WYOMING. The Southern Arapaho continued toward the Arkansas in southern COLORADO.

Although the tribe generally attempted to live in peace with whites, conflict inevitably arose, and the Arapahos took part in some of the best-known engagements of the INDIAN WARS. Whites had first encountered the tribe when it was living in the area of the BLACK HILLS, but settlement did not

An Arapaho Indian.

F. J. HAYNES PHOTO

Wyoming Arapahos meeting with President Chester A. Arthur in 1883.

encroach upon them until after 1840. The CALIFORNIA GOLD RUSH in 1849 brought increasing numbers of Euroamericans across their territory. In 1851, the Arapahos joined with other tribes in agreeing to allow roads and military outposts on their lands.

In 1864 seeking to clear the Plains of Indians, Colorado officials opened military operations against the Cheyennes and the Arapahos. Scattered fights took place. On November 29, 1864, a group of volunteers commanded by Colonel JOHN CHIVINGTON attacked a peaceful camp of Cheyennes and Arapahos on Sand Creek, killing 28 men and 105 women and children. Arapaho chief Left Hand was among the wounded. In January 1865, Cheyennes, Arapahos, and Sioux launched raids along a wide front to avenge the SAND CREEK MASSACRE.

More actions followed. Arapahos took part in the FETTERMAN Massacre in 1866. They were present at WASHITA in

An Arapaho Indian.

1868, when Custer attacked BLACK KETTLE's camp, coming to the aid of their Cheyenne allies. Some participated in the Battle of Adobe Walls with QUANAH PARKER's Comanches in 1874. They also took part in Custer's defeat at the LITTLE BIG HORN.

Eventually, the Southern Arapahos were confined to a reservation with the Southern Cheyennes in western Indian Territory. The Northern Arapahos moved to Wyoming's Wind River Reservation in Wyoming in 1876. Both bands were particularly active in the GHOST DANCE movement of 1889–1890.

ARIKARAS

The Arikaras are an Indian tribe of the Upper Missouri River region. When first encountered by the LEWIS AND CLARK EXPEDITION in 1804, the Arikaras lived in earth-covered lodges on the border of present-day North and South Dakota. In contrast to neighboring nomadic tribes, the Arikaras, a branch of the PAWNEES and similar in cultural patterns to the MANDANS, were farmers and BUFFALO hunters, semisettled "village Indians" known to mountain men as "Rickarees" or "Rees."

Originally hostile toward white explorers and traders, the Arikaras posed a significant obstacle to upriver travel on the MISSOURI RIVER, a circumstance that resulted in the most significant of all Indian-trapper encounters in the early history of the American West.

In the summer of 1823, WILLIAM ASHLEY and his recruited party of 70 BEAVER trappers (including many soon to become celebrated MOUNTAIN MEN: JEDEDIAH SMITH, JIM BRIDGER, HUGH GLASS, TOM FITZPATRICK, Jim Clyman, William and MILTON SUBLETTE) made their way from St. Louis to the Upper Missouri. On June 2, some 600 Arikaras attacked the party. They killed 15 of the trappers and wounded 12 others before forcing the Americans to retreat downstream. Ashley managed to get a message to FORT ATKINSON, NEBRASKA, about the inci-

An Arikara Indian.

dent. The result was the assembling in June 1823 of a 200-man punitive expedition of the Sixth Infantry led by Fort Atkinson's commander, Colonel Henry Leavenworth, a veteran of the War of 1812. His rather grandly named Missouri Legion, joined in their march upriver by some 700 SIOUX allies and numerous trapper volunteers from the MISSOURI FUR COMPANY, arrived at the Arikara village in August with a force of over 1,000 men. On August 14, after some preliminary skirmishing in which Leavenworth's field cannon were used effectively against the crudely barricaded lodges, the commander, in a decision later criticized by trappers and army authorities alike, allowed the Arikaras to abandon their village unpursued. The result of Leavenworth's perceived timidity was the damaging of white prestige among all the Upper Missouri tribes and the closing, for a time at least, of the river to the fur trade.

But the days of the Arikaras as an impediment to the river traffic were numbered. The tribe had already been decimated by disease epidemics in the 1770s, and in 1837 were again struck down by smallpox. The plague killed most of the Mandans and half of the neighboring Arikaras and Hidatsas (also known as the Minatarees), leaving an Arikara population of about 1,000.

In the 1850s, Arikara, Mandan, and Hidatsa (see GROS VENTRES) villages became important intertribal trading centers and the Arikaras had a more stable and friendly relationship with whites, many serving as scouts for the army in its Indian campaigns through the next quarter-century. (The most famous of the Arikara scouts was Bloody Knife, who in 1872 became a leader of the Arikaras attached to newly established Fort Abraham Lincoln in Dakota Territory. He became Lieutenant Colonel GEORGE ARMSTRONG CUSTER's favorite scout and was killed while serving with Major Marcus Reno's detachment in the BATTLE OF THE LITTLE BIG HORN on June 25, 1876.)

In 1900, about 400 Arikaras were living with Mandans and Hidatsas at Fort Berthold on the Missouri River. They eventually merged with those tribes, losing their cultural identity.

ARIZONA

The forty-eighth state in the Union, Arizona is known as "the Grand Canyon State." Arizona is marked by deserts and mountains. It is known to have been inhabited over 10,000 years ago by forebears of the PUEBLO, NAVAJO, and APACHE tribes. It is believed that the area was first irrigated for FARMING about 2,000 years ago.

From the mid-1500s through the late 1700s, Spanish explorers and missionaries traveled through this region. In 1736 silver was found near the northern Arizona Altar Valley region. The mines were exhausted within five years. This area was then known as Arizonac ("small spring"), which became the basis for the territory's name, Arizona.

By 1752, white settlers had established settlements in Arizona. Continued skirmishes with native dwellers led to the establishment of Fort Tucson in 1776. This protective stockade was noted for its thick ADOBE walls.

Arizona became part of MEXICO in 1821, when that coun-

LIBRARY OF CONGRESS

Artist Richard H. Kern painted these Arizona sandstone formations to look like man-made fortifications.

An aerial view of Phoenix, ca. 1890.

try achieved independence from Spain. In 1848, the region was ceded to the United States in the TREATY OF GUADALUPE HIDALGO, which ended the MEXICAN WAR. During the CIVIL WAR, Confederate troops occupied the land, claiming it as a Southern territory. Union forces were sent to defeat the Confederates, and Arizona was officially declared a United States territory in 1863.

As white settlers continued moving into the region, Navajo and Apache tribes fought the intrusion onto their lands. Despite numerous attacks, army troops ultimately defeated the Indian forces. In 1886, the Apache warrior GERONIMO finally surrendered, effectively bringing a close to the uprisings.

Arizona, with its rich veins of copper and other minerals, quickly became a site for widespread mining. As IRRIGATION techniques improved, the parched lands became fertile, and many ranchers chose to raise their stock in Arizona.

The move to make Arizona a state began in the 1890s. Although political squabbles held up the process for years, Arizona officially became the forty-eighth state on February 14, 1912.

Sprawling Fort Thomas, in the Arizona desert.

Arizona's landscape is divided into two main sections: the Colorado Plateau and the Basin and Range Region (see GREAT BASIN). The Colorado Plateau, in northern Arizona, encompasses about two-fifths of the state. The area is filled with many of the world's natural wonders, including the GRAND CANYON, the COLORADO RIVER, Monument Valley, the PETRIFIED FOREST, and the PAINTED DESERT. The Basin and Range Region, in the southern portion of the state, is known for its mountains and is more fertile, producing the majority of Arizona's crops, which include cotton, lettuce, melons, and oranges. Cattle ranching is Arizona's largest agricultural industry.

Arizona's numerous desert areas are filled with cacti. The mountainous regions support evergreens that include Ponderosa pines, blue spruce, and white fir. Animal life is abundant and extremely varied. Bears, bobcats, and mountain lions can be found in the Arizona forests; the deserts are home to rattlesnakes, Gila monsters, scorpions, and tarantulas. Doves, quail, and roadrunners are among Arizona's native birds.

ARKANSAS

The twenty-fifth state in the Union, Arkansas is known as "The Land of Opportunity." Arkansas takes its name from two sources: an Indian word meaning "downstream people," and the French word "Arkansas," their name for the Indian village Arkansea.

Arkansas is believed to have been settled originally by various Indian tribes, including the Caddos, OSAGES, Cherokees (see FIVE CIVILIZED TRIBES), Tulas, Chickasaws, Chickasawbas, and Quapaws. The first whites came to the area in the 1500s, when the Spanish explorer Hernando de Soto led his party into the Ozark Mountain region. A little over a century later, the French explorers Jacques Marquette and Louis Jolliet entered the Arkansas region after traveling down the MISSISSIPPI RIVER to the Arkansas River. French colonists began arriving in 1717, hoping to develop trapping and trading. These endeavors were unsuccessful, however.

After several skirmishes over the territory, Spain acquired Arkansas as part of the Louisiana Territory in 1763. In 1800, the area was turned over to the French and was obtained by the United States as part of the LOUISIANA PURCHASE in 1803. Congress declared Arkansas a U.S. territory in 1819, and a state on June 15, 1836.

As the CIVIL WAR loomed in 1860, Arkansas was divided over whether to join the Confederacy or remain in the Union.

In May 1861, the state voted to unite with the Southern states, though many Arkansas residents remained loyal to the Union. In 1864, following Little Rock's fall to Northern troops, Arkansas had two governments: one loyal to the Union, the other to the Confederacy. During the Reconstruction, Arkansas was governed by troops from the United States Army, until it was readmitted to the Union in 1868.

Much political turmoil ensued, and there were several violent outbreaks until President Grant intervened. Rapid growth followed in the 1880s, after rich bauxite mines opened near the state capital of Little Rock. The coming of the railroad and farming and industrial development were important to the state's economic expansion.

Arkansas has many lush areas for farming: cotton, soybeans, and rice are the leading crops. The state also has an abundance of forests—ranging from pines to hardwoods—

Arkansas pioneers as depicted in Harper's Weekly, *April 4, 1874.*

that cover about 50 percent of the land. The woods are home to a wide variety of animal species including deer, bobcats, muskrats, raccoons, and squirrels. Wild turkeys, geese, and ducks provided settlers with plenty of game for hunting.

The Arkansas landscape is diverse, from the Ozark Mountains to the rich valleys that surround the Arkansas River. Arkansas is also known for its natural springs, including the famed Hot Springs.

ASH HOLLOW MASSACRE

See GRATTAN MASSACRE

ASHLEY, WILLIAM HENRY
1778–1838

A Virginian who moved to Missouri about 1802, William Henry Ashley pursued careers in business, land speculation, the military, and politics before entering the fur business. He served on the frontier in the War of 1812 and by the early 1820s was lieutenant governor of the newly created state of Missouri and brigadier general of the state militia.

Although Ashley was not a "MOUNTAIN MAN" or a frontiersman, he became the most significant figure in the opening of the Rocky Mountain FUR TRADE. The famous newspaper notice of 1822 seeking "enterprising young men" for a fur-hunting expedition up the MISSOURI RIVER launched a brief but important career. In partnership with Andrew Henry, he established a post at the mouth of the Yellowstone River as a base for trapping the headwaters of the Missouri. His preference was to handle the supply and marketing aspects of the venture in St. Louis while Henry led the field parties, but in both 1822 and 1823 Ashley had to take the field as well. Both expeditions encountered Indian

Many famous mountain men responded to this ad placed in the St. Louis Missouri Gazette *in 1883.*

hostility, and the 1823 group suffered a disastrous defeat by ARIKARA Indians.

Previous initiatives had relied heavily on Indians to trap BEAVER and exchange skins for white manufactures. Ashley used white men, both free trappers and his own employees, to hunt BEAVER. Although this angered some Indian tribes, chiefly the militant BLACKFEET, it gave new vitality to the fur business and fixed its pattern for two decades. Blocked by Arikaras and Blackfeet on the Missouri, Ashley sent his trappers to the ROCKY MOUNTAINS and thus tapped a rich new hunting ground. The fur business thus became dependent on land rather than water transportation.

Twice more, between 1824 and 1826, Ashley himself took the field. On these journeys to the Rockies and beyond, he established a new system: the rendezvous and the annual supply caravan. Now trapping parties wintered in the fur country, conducted spring and fall hunts, and assembled at a designated rendezvous each summer to dispose of the year's catch, receive the next year's supplies, and rest and relax. In the spring, trains of pack mules brought the supplies from St. Louis, traveling the overland route up the Platte and across SOUTH PASS—a route that would become the OREGON TRAIL. After the rendezvous, the supply train returned laden with bales of BEAVER skins.

Having made a fortune at the rendezvous of 1826, near GREAT SALT LAKE, Ashley sold out to three of his associates: JEDEDIAH SMITH, David E. Jackson, and William Sublette. He had quickly perceived that the true profits of the fur business lay in supply and marketing rather than in trapping. He continued to supply the field parties from his St. Louis base while devoting himself to politics. Ashley ran unsuccessfully for governor of Missouri but was elected to the U.S. House of Representatives in 1831. Effectively championing western interests, he served until 1837. He died of pneumonia at the age of 60.

ASSINIBOINS

The Assiniboins are a Northern Plains tribe believed to have originated in the sixteenth century as a branch of the Yankton Dakotas (see SIOUX) with whom they share a dialect, and who allied the Crees and the Ojibwas (see CHIPPEWAS) of the Great Lakes region. In the seventeenth and eighteenth centuries, the Assiniboins, called Hohe by the Dakotas (who became their tribal enemies, along with the CROWS, BLACKFEET, and Atsinas), were located around Winnipeg, Manitoba, and in Saskatchewan. By 1850 the Assiniboins were found mostly along the MISSOURI RIVER north and west of the mouth of the Yellowstone; by the end of the century they numbered about 20,000.

In their winter camp at Fort Mandan on the upper Mis-

Wi-Jun-Jon, an Assiniboin chief, going to Washington and returning home, as depicted by George Catlin.

souri in 1804–1805, LEWIS AND CLARK met with an Assiniboin chief and several tribesmen. The explorers thought the Assiniboins a surly lot who mocked the MANDANS for their friendliness to the whites. But the Assiniboins, nomadic BUFFALO hunters and skilled traders among the other Plains tribes, themselves compiled a record of accord with whites while suffering greatly because of it. They were ravaged by smallpox around FORT UNION, the fur-trading post a few miles above the mouth of the Yellowstone, in the epidemic of 1837. So many died and were buried at the fort that when the cemetery was dug up in the early 1950s, the Assiniboin bones were taken away by the truckload, to be mixed with gravel to pave roads.

By 1843 the Assiniboin population had been reduced to about 4,000. With the Atsina (the GROS VENTRE of the Prairies) and Dakota tribes, the Assiniboins live today at Fort Peck and Fort Belknap in Montana.

LIBRARY OF CONGRESS

The skin lodge of an Assiniboin chief.

LIBRARY OF CONGRESS

The Assiniboins attacking the Blackfeet at Fort McKenzie. This draw-
ing, as well as the one above, was made by Karl Bodmer, one of few
artists to actually witness an Indian battle.

ASTOR, JOHN JACOB
1763–1848

John Jacob Astor, as painted by Gilbert Stuart.

Astor, a financier and FUR TRADE entrepreneur who founded the AMERICAN FUR COMPANY in 1808, dominated the fur business for decades. In 1821 he successfully lobbied Congress to abolish government trading posts, effectively opening up the fur trading business in the Plains and Rockies to private companies.

Astor was born on July 17, 1763, in Waldorf, Germany. In 1779 he went to London, where his brother was established as a manufacturer of flutes and other musical instruments. Astor worked with his brother for four years to gain mercantile experience and establish trade connections. He then traveled to America early in 1784 with a cargo of flutes which he sold in New York City. He used the profits from the sale to invest in furs; later that same year he returned to London and sold his furs at a profit. Intrigued by the fur business, he decided to return to America for good, and was back before the end of 1784.

After spending several years in New York City, Astor traveled to the Northwest when the British evacuated the area in 1796. The absence of the British meant that furs could be transported more easily to New York City and also enabled the Canadians to trade directly at American ports. In 1808, Astor founded the American Fur Company to challenge the British-Canadian trade along the northern border.

Two years later, he founded the Pacific Fur Company, but this venture failed during the War of 1812. After gaining control of the South West Company in 1817, he came to dominate the fur trade in the Northwest.

Astor sold the American Fur Company in 1834 and spent his later years in New York City, where he was also successful in real estate. He died in New York City on March 29, 1848, at the age of 84. At the time of his death, Astor was considered the wealthiest man in the country, with an estate reportedly worth $20 million. However, contemporary historians estimate that his net worth was closer to $8–$10 million.

ASTORIA

Astoria is a city in northwestern OREGON, seat of Clatsop County. LEWIS AND CLARK wintered at nearby Fort Clatsop in 1805–1806. Its location on the COLUMBIA RIVER estuary afforded them a view of the Pacific and a base from which they were able to explore the area before undertaking their journey back to Missouri.

In 1811, JOHN JACOB ASTOR's Pacific Fur Company established Fort Astoria, the first permanent U.S. settlement on the Pacific Coast. Although the post was sold to the North West Company of Montreal in 1813, its vigorous activities helped establish American claims to the Oregon Territory. Fort Astoria was returned to the United States in 1818, but trade, such as it was, remained in the hands of the British until the mid-1840s. In fact, Astoria had been somewhat superseded by FORT VANCOUVER as the center of the FUR TRADE in the Oregon country, and when American pioneers following the OREGON TRAIL reached it, they found little but the ruins of the old fort.

In 1847, the first U.S. post office on the Pacific Coast was

Fort Astoria, just before it fell into British hands.

established in Astoria. After the dispute over the Oregon boundary was settled with Great Britain in 1848, Astoria once again became a center of U.S. trading activity. The first customs district and port of entry were established two years later. The area was heavily settled by Scandinavian immigrants, and today its population includes many of their descendants. Fort Clatsop has been rebuilt as a National Memorial and is open to the public.

Stephen Fuller Austin.

along the Brazos, was 15 miles from the Gulf of Mexico and 175 miles from San Antonio. There Austin determined to build his town, San Felipe de Austin.

He soon expanded his plan for the American colony and petitioned the governor of the northern Mexican province of Coahuila y Texas for an enormous territory of about 18,000 square miles, estimating he could recruit 1,500 families to settle on the land and develop it. Toward the end of 1821, Austin was in New Orleans to raise capital for his Texas colony; with part of the money gained from selling interests in it, he bought a sloop, the *Lively,* and stocked it with tools and equipment. The vessel ran aground on Galveston Island and was a total loss. The indefatigable Austin immediately returned to his colony. When he arrived in January 1822, he found several settlers had preceded him and built cabins on the land.

Until 1830, Austin managed his domain without significant interference from Mexico City. He was first of all loyal to Mexico, and in addition established a sound legal and court system for the colony, had the land grant carefully surveyed, encouraged trade agreements with the United States, supervised the building of schools and of mills for processing cotton and lumber, and organized local militia to fight marauding Indians—the Karankawas in particular.

In 1830, when Austin's colonies around San Felipe had a population of about 4,000 (about one-quarter the number of Americans in Texas), the Mexican government passed laws attempting to slow Anglo immigration to Texas. In 1833, Texans at the San Felipe Convention drew up a constitution for a proposed independent state government of Texas; Austin was asked to take it to Mexico City, to President Antonio López de Santa Anna. For his efforts Austin was imprisoned briefly in the Mexican capital. In August 1835 he returned to Texas and found the Americans there on the verge of revolution.

In October 1835, Austin served as commander of the Texas Army in San Antonio, then was selected as a commissioner to travel to Washington to seek U.S. recognition of the Republic of Texas. He returned in June 1836, and after defeat by SAM HOUSTON for election as first president of Texas, retired to his cabin on the Brazos, alone (he never married), ill, impoverished, and adrift. Houston saved him from bitterness and humiliation by appointing him as the Republic's secretary of state, an office he held until his death on December 27, 1836. Houston, in announcing Austin's death, said, "The father of Texas is no more."

B

BACA, ELFEGO
1865–1945

Sheriff, lawyer, and politician, Elfego Baca was one of the most colorful Mexican-American folk heroes of the nineteenth century, and the survivor of one of the West's more storied gun battles. Born in Socorro, New Mexico, he was educated in Topeka, Kansas, until age 15, when his father brought him back to Socorro. The elder Baca was then town marshal at nearby Belen, New Mexico. He was jailed after killing two cowboys, but his son helped him escape.

At 19, Baca, serving as a self-appointed special deputy at Frisco, New Mexico, got into a fight with hands from the Texas-based John B. Slaughter ranch who apparently had been using local Mexicans and their herds for target practice. The next day, Baca found himself cornered in a small shack by an army of vengeance-seeking cowboys, some 80 in number. Miraculously, after a 36-hour siege in which some 4,000 shots were fired, Baca, having killed four and wounded eight of his pursuers, was allowed to surrender to a friendly deputy sheriff. He was twice tried and acquitted in Albuquerque on murder charges stemming from the incident.

An instant folk hero among the MEXICAN-AMERICAN population of the region, Baca was ensured of a long and fruitful political career. He was admitted to the bar in 1894 after reading law with a local judge, and won elections for deputy sheriff, country clerk, mayor, district attorney, sheriff, and Socorro County superintendent of schools. He continued to work as a lawyer and private detective almost until his death in 1945.

BANCROFT, HUBERT HOWE
1832–1918

Hubert Howe Bancroft was a bookseller and publisher, and one of the first historians to chronicle life in the trans-Mississippi West. Books were always at the center of Bancroft's life, from his first job as an assistant in his brother-in-law's bookstore in Buffalo, until his death. His brother-in-law, George Derby, suspected that one could make

Bancroft employed many assistants in writing his history of the North American West. Their disembodied arms are shown in this 1885 cartoon.

a fortune in the CALIFORNIA GOLD RUSH even without a pick and shovel, and in February 1852, he dispatched Bancroft to the West Coast with $5,000 worth of books and stationery.

After a false start in SACRAMENTO and a brief return east, Bancroft settled and prospered in SAN FRANCISCO, establishing his own firm with his brother Albert. Under the names H. H. Bancroft and Company, A. L. Bancroft Company, and the Bancroft Company, they expanded into publishing. By 1870, theirs was the largest book and stationery house west of Chicago.

Bancroft's crowning achievement was his multivolume *The History of the Pacific States of North America,* which ultimately reached 39 volumes. Bancroft wrote four volumes in the set and edited most of the others. He sold his own library, consisting of more than 60,000 manuscripts and books, to the University of California in 1905, and continued to write on both historical and contemporary topics until his death.

BANNOCKS

The Bannocks are a Uzo-Aztecan tribe of Indians related to the Shoshone and living in southeastern IDAHO.

During the eighteenth century, the Bannocks migrated from eastern OREGON into Idaho, settling along the Snake and Salmon rivers. They also ranged into western WYOMING. Those living along the Salmon River were encountered by LEWIS AND CLARK in 1805 and probably were referred by them as the Broken Moccasin tribe.

In 1868, by the Treaty of Fort Bridger, the Bannocks agreed to accept a RESERVATION on the upper SNAKE RIVER. They were careful, however, to reserve exclusive rights to an area known as Camas Prairie, a significant site where the lilylike camas plant, an important part of the Bannock diet, grew.

Food was scarce on the new reservation, and the Bannocks turned to BUFFALO hunting with the blessing of their Indian agent. Chronic shortages still occurred, however, and the camas root became even more important to the tribe. In the spring of 1878, the people moved to Camas Prairie, where they found white settlers who had been encroaching on the area for several years. The Bannock chief, Buffalo Horn, ordered the outsiders off the Indians' land. In the ensuing confusion, some of the whites were shot. Though some of the Indians involved returned immediately to the reservation, others fled. Pursued by Army units under O. O. HOWARD and NELSON MILES, they were rounded up. A few escaped to Wyoming, where in September they were attacked and massacred, their attempts to surrender ignored.

BARBED WIRE

Fencing material made out of twisted wire with spaced, coiled barbs played a decisive role in the transition of the West from open plains to enclosed pastures and irrevocably altered the society and economy of the region. Before the invention of cheap man-made material, fences were constructed from whatever natural materials were at hand: stone barriers where stone was plentiful, wooden barricades where forests predominated. In the East, fencing was used to protect crops from grazing animals. In the West, however, there were prairies with few rocks or trees, and the cattle required large open ranges for feeding. The unwritten law of the OPEN RANGE allowed free access to vast areas that provided water and grass. Agricultural interests, on the other hand, demanded enclosed areas for maximum crop yield. Farmers, who were not in the business of raising crops to

Wire cutting on a Nebraska ranch, a common practice during the range wars.

feed grazing cows, squared off against the cattlemen, insisting that the latter be responsible for the very expensive proposition of confining their stock. Inventive farmers began to use the osage orange plant, a hardy natural hedging material, that could thrive in various soils.

After the Civil War, demand for meat increased, and by 1870 the buffalo had been hunted to near extinction. Beef was the answer, and the clash between farmers and cowmen escalated into open warfare. A number of inventors had recognized the need for cheap and easily manufactured fencing material, but it was not until 1873 that a DeKalb, Illinois, farmer, JOSEPH FARWELL GLIDDEN, found a solution. Patent number 157,124, issued November 24, 1874, was for a machine that could produce wired barbs entwined by double-strand wires. Glidden began manufacture the same year. Patent refinements led to production of a great variety of wires—single cable, double cable, round, and half-round— across a range of gauges. Barbed-wire production skyrocketed, and between 1875 and 1885 annual production increased from under 300 tons to 100,000 tons. So widespread was the use of barbed wire that by 1890 the open range in the West was nearly all fenced pastureland. Cattle was no longer king; ranchers could isolate their stock and control breeding, and the long drives were supplanted by the railroad that moved the cattle safely and quickly to market, with less weight loss. Homesteaders benefited from this sectioning off of the Great Plains, and as a result, agriculture, settlements, and commerce combined to forge an economy more powerful than either cattlemen or farmers would ever have dreamed.

BARTLETT, JOHN RUSSELL
1805–1886

Although his work to determine the boundary between the United States and MEXICO following the TREATY OF GUADALUPE HIDALGO (1848) was largely a failure, John Russell Bartlett wrote a detailed personal narrative of his work that is regarded as a classic of southwestern history.

He was born in Providence, Rhode Island, and spent his youth in Ontario. In 1836 he moved to New York City and opened a bookstore, which he ran until 1850. Bartlett's study of American Indian ethnology resulted in his cofounding (in 1842) of the American Ethnological Society and the publication of his first books, *Progress in Ethnology* (1847) and *Dictionary of Americanisms* (1848).

In June 1850, Bartlett, probably through his Whig political connections, was appointed commissioner of the U.S.–Mexico Boundary Survey; in November he arrived in El Paso with a large entourage of civilians and an 85-man military escort to begin his assigned work. Bartlett's predecessors—Ambrose Sevier, John B. Weller, and JOHN C. FRÉMONT—had left unresolved most of the decisions on the critical portion of the boundary from the RIO GRANDE westward. The new commissioner and his Mexican counterpart,

A Bartlett sketch of California Indians gambling inside an earth-covered council house.

General Pedro García Condé, quickly came to grips with two serious flaws in the map used by the Guadalupe–Hidalgo Treaty negotiators: a latitude error placing El Paso del Norte (modern Juárez, Mexico, across the Rio Grande from El Paso, Texas) 34 miles too far north and a longitude error placing the Rio Grande 100 miles too far east. These lapses complicated the status of the SANTA RITA copper mines and the settlement of Mesilla and its fertile farming valley, both in New Mexico Territory, and a proposed transcontinental railroad route.

The Bartlett-Condé Compromise, worked out toward the end of 1850, in effect gave latitude to the Mexican government, and longitude to the Americans; Bartlett sacrificed Mesilla and the railroad route to protect the copper mines. The compromise was the subject of strong criticism among Bartlett's surveying party and among expansionist Democrats at odds with Whig President Millard Fillmore.

As disputes deepened—the Bartlett-Condé "line" was repudiated in Washington and a new surveyor, Captain

William H. Emory, arrived to take over the work from El Paso west—Bartlett set out for SAN DIEGO to recommence the boundary work from west to east. After recovering from cholera and making a leisurely trip through northern Sonora and from San Diego to SAN FRANCISCO and back, he resumed command of the boundary commission in May 1852. He and his party traveled east along the GILA RIVER to the Rio Grande, with side trips to Tucson and Chihuahua, reaching El Paso in August.

By now, however, Bartlett's leadership and his long absences from commission work had been roundly criticized along the border and in Washington. In January 1853 he left the Southwest to return to his native Providence. The boundary work continued until 1853, when James Gadsden's mission to Mexico resulted in the GADSDEN PURCHASE, which ended the Rio Grande–westward boundary dispute and gave the United States its coveted railroad right-of-way and the Mesilla Valley. Bartlett published his invaluable history in 1854 and the following year was elected Rhode Island's secretary of state, an office he held until 1872. Among his many published works is a 10-volume history of Rhode Island through 1792.

BASIN AND RANGE PROVINCE

See GREAT BASIN

BASKETRY

For thousands of years, a remarkable variety of baskets have been made by Indian tribes throughout the United States. Many different barks, grasses, leaves, rushes, and other plants are used, depending on the tribe and the purpose of the basket. Some tribes of the Far West and the Northwest produced hats and caps of woven basketry.

Although Native American baskets are often very beautiful, they were never made simply to be decorative; they were, in fact, essential to the survival of the people. Baskets were everyday household items, used as carriers, platters, bowls, and storage containers for food and seeds. When woven tightly (and sometimes caulked with substances such as resin), baskets could even be used to hold and store water.

Some of the best-known examples of basketry among western tribes are those produced by the PAIUTES, Papagos, Pimas, and Pomos. Intricate symbolic designs often were

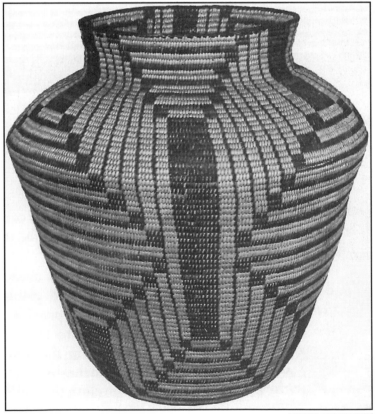

DENVER ART MUSEUM

A Pima storage basket.

SMITHSONIAN INSTITUTION

A Paiute woman wearing a grass basket outside her brush hut.

woven into the baskets. Among the Pomos of CALIFORNIA, basketry was an integral part of their culture. Strict rules
applied to the collection of materials and the weaving of the
basket. Designs and techniques were handed down matrilin-
eally. Traditional basketmaking also related to prophecy and

A Paiute water bottle.

power. Mabel McKay, the last of the traditional Pomo weavers, pointed out the religious aspect of the weavers' work, saying that the details of every basket she made—the design, shape, and use—came to her in dreams.

BASQUE SETTLERS IN THE WEST

The Basques originally came from an area in the western Pyrenees Mountains, located along the Bay of Biscay, within both Spain and France. They had their own culture and language, and faced many prejudices after migrating to the American West. Other settlers viewed them as a closed community of outsiders. Many Basques settled around Boise, IDAHO, and a large Basque population remains there today.

The Basques, along with Hispanic and Mormon settlers, became known for their sheep ranches, which expanded throughout the West in the 1870s. Unfortunately, this growth brought problems with cattle ranchers, many of whom felt that the herds of these foreigners destroyed the rangelands for cattle.

NEVADA HISTORICAL SOCIETY

Basque cowboys and sheepherders at the Pioneer Saloon in McDermitt, Nevada, around 1900.

MERCALDO ARCHIVES, UNIVERSITY OF TEXAS

Sam Bass.

BASS, SAM
1851–1878

Sam Bass was a notorious outlaw whose bank and train robberies terrorized citizens in TEXAS, NEBRASKA, and the Dakota Territory. Betrayed by a member of his own gang, Bass was fatally shot by the TEXAS RANGERS, and died on his twenty-seventh birthday.

Bass was born on July 21, 1851, in Indiana, and reared by an uncle. At age 18 he went to Denton, Texas, where he worked as a farmhand for Sheriff W. F. Eagan. In 1874, Bass purchased a racehorse and, with it, success. He quit his job and began life as a gambler. In 1875, after winning some ponies at Fort Sill, Indian Territory, Bass took them and a number of others and fled to San Antonio, Texas. It was his first known robbery.

Later he befriended Joel Collins, and they began a freight line operation out of Deadwood, Dakota Territory. They soon sold it to buy a saloon and casino, and finally a mine. Eventually broke, Bass decided to make his money as a robber. He led several desperadoes in seven successful STAGECOACH robberies before leaving the BLACK HILLS. On September 18, 1877, Bass and outlaws James Berry, Jack Davis, Bill Heffridge, and Tom Nixon seized more than $60,000 during a train robbery at Big Spring, Nebraska. Within a few weeks, Heffridge, Berry, and Joel Collins were shot, but Bass escaped to Texas and organized another gang.

In the spring of 1878, Bass and his bandits staged four

train holdups around Dallas. His former employer, Sheriff Eagan, joined the manhunt for the gang. That summer, Bass planned a bank robbery in Round Rock, Texas. But Jim Murphy, a gang member who later shot himself, betrayed him to the Texas Rangers in exchange for leniency. Ranger George Harrel shot Bass during a bloody clash in the streets of Round Rock, and he died two days later.

BEADLE, ERASTUS

See DIME NOVELS

UNIVERSITY OF OKLAHOMA LIBRARY

Judge Roy Bean.

BEAN, ROY
ca. 1827–1903

Bean's life is so inextricably mixed with folklore and myth that even his most assiduous biographer, C. L. Sonnichsen, had to be content to deal briskly with the few historical facts and devote the balance of his book to Bean tales, of which there is an endless supply.

Roy Bean was born in Mason County, Kentucky, between 1825 and 1830 and spent the first 30 years of his life—if one takes his word and that of the sparse other evidence—in and out of trouble with the law. In 1848, with his brother Sam, he is believed to have trafficked in trade goods on the SANTA FE TRAIL. He then made his way to MEXICO, where he killed a man and fled to CALIFORNIA. In

Judge Roy Bean served liquor along with justice at his saloon/court-house in Langtry.

San Diego, where another brother, Joshua, operated a saloon, Bean fought a duel in 1852. He was jailed but escaped and went to San Gabriel, north of Los Angeles. Joshua Bean, who either preceded or followed his brother, opened a saloon in San Gabriel and ran it successfully until he was murdered, for reasons not known, in the mid-1850s. Roy took over the saloon and did well with it until, by his own account, he was nearly lynched for courting a Spanish girl from a prominent local family. The girl's other suitor and his friends actually strung him up, Bean said, but the rope was too long; and as he clung to life, his toes touching the ground, the young woman he had fought over cut him down. (He did, contemporaries said, have a scar around his neck, and could not turn his head independently of his upper body.)

In NEW MEXICO Territory, and later in SAN ANTONIO, Bean served with volunteer Confederate irregulars during the CIVIL WAR. He remained in San Antonio for 16 years after the war, married, and worked in the saloon trade. In 1882, Bean left his wife and children, and in a wagon loaded with whiskey and other trade goods, traveled to the junction of the Pecos and Rio Grande, where he opened a tent saloon. In July of that year he moved his operation to Eagle's Nest Springs on the Rio Grande; he named the place Langtry and the saloon the Jersey Lilly, after the English beauty and actress LILLIE LANGTRY, with whom he became infatuated after seeing her photograph. He liked to say she was an "acquaintance," he subscribed to theatrical magazines to follow her career and clip pictures of her, and he steadfastly defended her honor. Sadly, he was never to meet her.

In August 1882, Bean was appointed justice of the peace and, except for one term, served in that capacity (which he called the "Law West of the Pecos") until 1902, administering justice and serving liquor, often simultaneously, at the Jersey Lilly.

Among the countless tales, many of them well documented, of Bean's antic administration of justice are these: He once fined a lawyer for using profane language in his court when the lawyer announced he intended to use habeas corpus in defending his client. He assessed a fine of $20 on a saloon patron who said the picture of Lillie Langtry "looked like a range heifer." He sentenced rustlers and horse thieves to be hanged "pronto," and often ended his verdict by ordering that the culprit's neck "be tied to a limb in some open place where his cronies will be sure to see him." He granted quick divorces to couples whose marriages (which he had performed) did not "take hold." And once, after inspecting the corpse of a railroader who had fallen from a bridge, fined the victim the $40 he had in his pocket "for carrying a concealed weapon" and confiscated the pistol "for use by the court."

Bean died in his room in the Jersey Lilly on March 16, 1903.

BEAR FLAG REPUBLIC
1846

The United States had a long history of coveting Alta (Upper, as opposed to Baja, Lower) CALIFORNIA before the MEXICAN WAR delivered it into American hands. President Andrew Jackson had proposed buying it, and James Polk made its acquisition one of the principal aims of his presidency. In 1846, the great Mexican province lay virtually ungoverned and undefended: only four presidios were strung along its coast, each ill-equipped, ill-armed, and under-manned; the entire population of the province was under 4,000, including about 800 Anglos.

Before the news of the outbreak of the war with Mexico reached the Pacific, an American rebellion was beginning in the northern part of Alta California, centered around the Sacramento Valley, where the Swiss-born entrepreneur JOHN AUGUSTUS SUTTER had built a fort and, deeply in debt, was encouraging American immigration by offering parcels of the 50,000 acres he held under a Mexican land grant.

In December 1845, Captain JOHN C. FRÉMONT, leading an expedition, rode into Sutter's Fort, then continued south to Monterey, where he informed Mexican officials he was exploring a route to the Oregon Territory. Frémont was permitted to winter in California but was warned to stay inland, away from the settled coastal areas. He defied the order, and Colonel José Castro, commander of Mexican forces in the northern part of the province, gathered his cavalry and forced an infuriated Frémont and his men to abandon their California mission and proceed into Oregon. During the march north, Frémont and his party, which included the American consul in California, Thomas O. Larkin, were discovered on May 9, 1846, at Klamath Lake by a U.S. Marine Corps lieutenant, Archibald Gillespie. An agent and courier for President Polk, Gillespie had confidential dispatches from Washington for Larkin and Frémont that resulted in Frémont's return to Sutter's Fort. (Although the United States did not declare war against Mexico until May 13, Zachary Taylor had massed his forces on the RIO GRANDE in late March and had fought two battles against the Mexicans by the time Gillespie met the Frémont party. It seems clear that the messages from Polk had to do with the impending war.)

Frémont and his men arrived at Sutter's Fort on June 9. The next day the first overt move toward establishing the short-lived Bear Flag Republic was made. A group of Sacramento Valley settlers, led by Ezekiel Merritt, a trapper described by H. H. Bancroft as "a coarse-grained, loud-mouthed, unprincipled, whiskey-drinking, quarrelsome fellow," ambushed a Mexican officer and nine men who were leading 170 horses to Castro at Santa Clara. Merritt and his raiders left the Mexicans with one horse each, and took the remaining herd back to Sutter's Fort.

Four days later, with Frémont's sanction, Merritt took men and headed south to seize Sonoma and the north SAN FRANCISCO Bay area. On June 14, the raiders captured the local military commander, Colonel Mariano G. Vallejo (who was, ironically, strongly pro-American and a supporter of U.S. annexation of California) and his family, informed them they were prisoners of war, and removed them to Sutter's Fort. There, Frémont, still smarting over his humiliating expulsion earlier that year, ordered the family jailed.

Meantime, with Sonoma as its capital, the Republic of California was created in a proclamation drafted by William B. Ide, a Vermont-born carpenter and farmer who declared the new government would overthrow the Mexican "military despotism." A newcomer to California, William Todd (a cousin of Mary Todd Lincoln), made the declaration official by presenting the crude flag he had fashioned, depicting a grizzly bear, a red star, and the words "California Republic" on a white field. Thereafter the revolutionaries were known as Bear Flaggers.

Ide and his men, including Americans who came to join them after the proclamation was distributed as far south as Monterey, prepared to defend Sonoma against an expected attack by Castro's army, heading north from San Francisco.

A small skirmish occurred on June 24 at Olompali, a rancho near present-day Novato, in which a Mexican force suffered one killed and several wounded, and the Americans escaped unscathed. A day later, Frémont's command of 90 men arrived in Sonoma to help defend it and captured the nearby settlement of San Rafael. On July 1, having sailed down the coast in an American merchant ship, Frémont and his men entered San Francisco, spiked an ancient Spanish cannon at San Joaquin (at the south entrance to San Francisco Bay), and occupied the presidio. On Independence Day, at a huge banquet and celebration, Frémont announced the creation of the California Battalion of Volunteers, which he would command with Gillespie as his adjutant.

As this military unit was being formally organized, however, events in the south were to end the need for Frémont's battalion and, indeed, for the Bear Flag Republic. On July 2, 1846, Commodore John D. Sloat of the U.S. Navy, who had dispatched two ships ahead of him, sailed into Monterey Bay on his flagship, *Savannah,* and on July 7 occupied Monterey, raising the American flag over California. On July 9, when the news of the American occupation of California was carried to Sonoma by Lieutenant Joseph W. Revere, grandson of Paul Revere, the Bear Flag was lowered from its mast in the public plaza and the Bear Flag Republic came to an end 30 days after its creation.

BEAVER

A member of the rodent family found chiefly in North America, the beaver was highly prized by Western trappers and furriers for its pelt.

Adult beavers are three to four feet long, and can weigh anywhere from 30 to 70 pounds. They have thick brown fur, a humped back, and a long, flat tail that measures about a foot long and six inches thick. This unique appendage serves as a rudder when beavers are swimming and helps the beaver balance when standing on its hind legs. Young beavers, called "kits" or "pups," are born in litters of two to four. The average life span of a beaver is 12 years.

Beavers were trapped for fur and meat. Both white trappers and Indians used the pelts for clothing. A Western trapper named Jim Baird wrote, "beaver is the most precious

Reports by scouts and explorers of abundant beaver led to a boom in the fur-trapping business.

product this territory produces." From the mid-1600s through the late 1800s, beaver pelts were a valuable commodity for traders. In one 24-year period, the HUDSON'S BAY COMPANY shipped over 3 million of them to London for use by coat and hat manufacturers. On the frontier, beaver pelts were as good as money. Traders bartered them for ammunition and knives, cooking utensils, tobacco, and blankets. Twelve beaver pelts was the going rate in trade for one rifle.

People writing about the new western frontier were fascinated by the beaver, which was portrayed as an industrious creature living in a harmonious social order. Beavers were also depicted as fierce warriors. Enraged beavers would, the stories claimed, bite off the tails of any other beaver that dared to intrude on their territory. This, wrote one individual, was "the greatest disgrace to which a beaver can be exposed."

Because of the high demand for beaver pelts, the creatures were in danger of extinction by the late 1800s. Government officials in both the United States and Canada passed measures protecting wild beavers in North America. (See also FUR TRADE.)

BECKNELL, WILLIAM
1788–1865

Called the "father of the SANTA FE TRAIL," William Becknell was born in Amherst County, Virginia, and moved to Franklin, Missouri, as a young man. He served in the War of 1812.

After the overthrow of Spanish power in NEW MEXICO in 1821, Becknell and four others went West in hopes of trading goods. After a relatively swift journey (only five months), he sold his goods in TAOS and SANTA FE at a huge profit. Encouraged by the financial success and speed of his first endeavor, Becknell advertised the following spring for 70 men to join him on another expedition. With 30 volunteers, he left Missouri on August 4, 1822, with $5,000 in merchandise. They arrived in Santa Fe on November 16, having taken a new route that departed from the Arkansas River near present-day Dodge City and crossed to the Cimarron. Their new route, dubbed the Santa Fe Trail, quickly became the accepted trade route for the prairie.

Becknell led at least one more party to New Mexico, then an 1824 trapping expedition to western Colorado and eastern Utah. He commanded a militia company in the BLACK HAWK WAR and, in late 1835, led a group to Texas to take part in the War of Independence against Mexico. He settled near Clarksville, Texas, and remained there until his death in 1865.

BECKWOURTH, JAMES P.
1798–1866

James Pierson, Beckwourth was born at Fredericksburg, Virginia to a mulatto mother and white father. The family later moved to St. Charles, Missouri, where he was apprenticed to a blacksmith.

In 1824, Beckwourth joined WILLIAM H. ASHLEY and Andrew Henry on a fur-trapping expedition in the Rockies. He became an experienced trapper, going out with Ashley and others on several occasions in the mid-1820s. During those expeditions, he skirmished with the BLACKFEET and other Indians.

In 1828, Beckwourth decided to join the CROWS, who welcomed him warmly. He married a succession of Crow women and claims to have acquitted himself admirably as a member of war parties during his six years with the Crow nation. In the summer of 1835, he joined another expedition, this time to California. Beckwourth fought in the SEMINOLE War under Zachary Taylor. Subsequently, he returned to the West,

Jim Beckwourth.

where he participated in the 1845 California insurrection and the CHEYENNE War of 1864.

Beckwourth met an ex-newspaperman, T. D. Bonner, who helped him write an autobiography, which was published in 1856. The reliability of that book is highly questionable; as one historian has observed, "Beckwourth was probably the biggest liar west of the Mississippi." Beckwourth finally settled in Colorado among the Crows. When he died, he was buried as a Crow, on a tree platform.

BEECHER'S ISLAND, BATTLE OF
1868

In this battle Major GEORGE A. FORSYTH and 50 of his men were besieged by CHEYENNES and SIOUX, and trapped on Beecher's Island for eight days. In August 1868 many of the Cheyennes were camped along the Arikara fork of the Republican River in Colorado. General PHILIP SHERIDAN dispatched Forsyth and a group of scouts to search out the Indian camps. On September 16, a Sioux hunting party spotted Forsyth's company and alerted their people, as well as the Cheyenne camp, that their hunting ground had been invaded. The following day, about 600 Cheyennes and Sioux warriors traveled down the Arikara valley toward Forsyth's camp. When the Indians charged, the soldiers held them off with their Spencer repeating rifles and then took refuge on a small island. The Indian warriors surrounded Forsyth's men and held them in siege for eight days. Two couriers, Jack Stillwell and Pierre Trudeau, finally managed to slip out at night and summoned aid from the 10th Cavalry.

Forsyth lost about 20 of his men during the battle. The island on which the battle took place was named after one of the men killed there, Lieutenant Frederick Beecher, and the fight became known as the Battle of Beecher's Island.

The Battle of Beecher Island.

Forsyth's men exaggerated the significance of the fight and boasted of killing hundreds of Indians. However, according to Native American accounts the number killed was less than 30. The death of the great warrior ROMAN NOSE, however, was a tremendous loss for the Cheyennes.

BELL, PHILIP ALEXANDER
1809–1889

Although he is all but forgotten today, Alexander Philip Bell wrote one of the most important early chapters in AFRICAN-AMERICAN journalism. Little is known about his early life, but in 1831 he burst on the scene as secretary of a group of "colored citizens" of New York opposed to the Colonization Society and its program of repatriating black Americans to Africa. He was active in numerous other black and interracial organizations and a member of the American Anti-Slavery Society. Bell was an advocate of black self-help programs, and also a staunch antisegregationist.

In 1837 he began publishing a newspaper, the *Weekly Advocate,* with Samuel Cornish as its editor. The second African-American newspaper to be published, it lasted only three months, when it became the *Colored American.* Bell edited the paper under that name until 1839.

His activities for the next several years are unknown, but he re-emerged in San Francisco in 1857. In 1862 he became co-editor of the *Pacific Appeal,* a weekly black newspaper of considerable repute. Finally, in 1865, Bell started another newspaper, *The Elevator.* Both his West Coast journalistic ventures were of high quality, but the readership was undoubtedly too small to sustain them. Bell later became doorkeeper of the CALIFORNIA state senate. He is believed to have died in dire poverty.

MERCALDO ARCHIVES, UNIVERSITY OF TEXAS

Charles Bent.

BENT, CHARLES
1799–1847

Charles Bent was a highly successful Virginia-born fur trader and businessman who operated chiefly in Colorado and New Mexico. After the MEXICAN WAR he was appointed the first American governor of the New Mexico Territory. The eldest of four brothers, he sought adventure and profit in the FUR TRADE. After a likely stint with JOHN JACOB ASTOR's AMERICAN FUR COMPANY he joined the MISSOURI FUR COMPANY in 1822, becoming a partner in 1825. Severe competition led to the failure of the company, and Bent left MISSOURI to trade along the SANTA FE TRAIL with his 20-year-old brother, William, in 1829. The brothers and CERAN ST. VRAIN organized Bent, St. Vrain and Company in 1831; it soon became the largest trading company in the Southwest, with markets in Taos and Santa Fe.

In 1833, to consolidate Indian trade routes on the Arkansas River, the trio built BENT'S FORT north of the juncture of the Purgatoire and Arkansas Rivers in Colorado. From this mountain site the company controlled trade in blankets, BUFFALO robes, sheep, horses, mules, and the vital Indian fur trade. William was left to run Bent's Fort, and in 1837 the construction of Fort St. Vrain on the South Platte River further extended the company's control.

Charles left for the Mexican province of New Mexico and settled in Taos in 1835. His interest was in land speculation. He married the Mexican governor's daughter, and after the conquest of New Mexico in the MEXICAN WAR of 1846, Charles, through his wealth, prominence, and American heritage, became the first American governor of the province. However, his overbearing manner and harsh tongue had earned him enemies, and in a revolt by Mexican and Taos Indians Charles was killed and scalped.

BENT, WILLIAM

See BENT'S FORT.

William Bent with Arapaho Chief Little Raven (left) and his family.

BENT'S FORT

Built in 1833 by the hugely successful fur-trading firm of Bent, St. Vrain and Company 12 miles upstream from the junction of the Purgatoire and Arkansas Rivers in Colorado, Bent's Fort commanded the trading routes north and south along the Platte River and east and west along the SANTA FE TRAIL. CHARLES BENT, his brother William, and CERAN ST. VRAIN were the principals in the trading company. William oversaw the construction, which has led to some confusion about the fort's name—it was commonly known as Bent's Fort, frequently also as Fort William, and later as Bent's Old Fort. From this strategic mountain trading post—the best-known and largest of the period—furs, livestock, and other commodities flowed overland between Indians and whites. Before and during the MEXICAN WAR the fort served as supply depot for military maneuvers.

William became the sole owner of the company after St. Vrain's retirement in 1849. Charles had sought other interests

Exterior and interior views of Bent's Fort.

in the Mexican province of NEW MEXICO; he settled in TAOS in 1835, became the first appointed American governor of the province in 1846, and was killed in an Indian rebellion in January 1847. William thought he could profitably sell the fort to the United States, but the government offered what he believed was an insultingly low price. Angered, he blew up the fort in 1849. In 1853 William built Bent's New Fort 38 miles downstream from the junction of the Purgatoire and Arkansas Rivers, and in 1859 he leased the new fort to the government. William Bent died in 1869. (See also FUR TRADE.)

BENTON, THOMAS HART
1782–1858

CHICAGO HISTORICAL SOCIETY

Thomas Hart Benton.

Thomas Hart Benton, born near Hillsborough, North Carolina, was a political writer, U.S. senator, leader of the Democratic Party during the Jackson era, and steadfast proponent of agrarian causes and westward expansion. The oldest of eight children, he redeemed the debt-ridden family estate after his father's death in 1791. After a series of youthful misadventures, several of a violent nature, Benton became a lawyer in 1806 and a Tennessee state legislator in 1809. He served in the War of 1812, but his temper got him into a brawl with General Andrew Jackson, whom Benton shot. Benton then moved to Missouri, where he killed a man in a duel. He served as editor (1818–1826) of the *Missouri Enquirer* and advocated a larger economic role for the West and for the United States through trade with the Far East.

In 1820 Benton was elected as one of the first U.S. senators from Missouri; he gained recognition as an unflappable spokesman for rapid westward settlement and commercial and agrarian development. He championed claims to Spanish and French land grants, and pursued development of the Rocky Mountain fur trade, and the construction of a national road, canal, and rail system linking East with West. As chairman of the Committee on Indian Affairs he was responsible for removing the Creek Indians from their land in Georgia so that whites could settle on it. In 1835 Benton and Andrew Jackson made up their differences; Benton became a leader of the Democratic Party and supported Jackson's dissolution of the Second Bank of the United States.

Although Benton was a slave owner and pro-Southern, he came to the conclusion that slavery should not be extended to the western territories for several reasons: the geography of the West was unsuited to that institution; slavery would not lead to full and proper national growth; and its spread would prove perilous for maintaining the Union. As the sectional controversy between slave and nonslave interests increased, Benton became unpopular; he lost his Senate seat in 1850, won a seat in the House of Representatives for the 1853–55 term, and lost his bid for the governorship in 1856. He rejected the newly founded Republican Party and even spoke against the Republican presidential nominee, his son-in-law JOHN C. FRÉMONT.

The ex-politician and advocate of MANIFEST DESTINY was not embittered by the turn of events; he devoted the last years of his life to legal and political writings. His *Thirty Years' View* was a two-volume historical account of the U.S. government from 1820 to 1850; *Examination* refuted the Supreme Court ruling on the 1857 DRED SCOTT DECISION; and his 16-volume *Abridgement of the Debates of Congress* encompassed the years 1789 to 1856.

BIERCE, AMBROSE
1842–ca. 1914

CALIFORNIA HISTORICAL SOCIETY

Ambrose Gwinnet Bierce.

Ambrose Bierce was a journalist and short story writer, notorious in the West for his sarcasm and quick wit. Born in Ohio, Bierce served as a Union Army officer during the CIVIL WAR. He later trekked to San Francisco, where his contributions to the *Overland Monthly* and other local papers launched his career. As editor of the *News-Letter,* Bierce's satirical column of verse and commentary gained statewide attention. Although he spent many years in London and Washington, D.C., Bierce maintained a feisty presence in western publications. His "Prattle" column in the San Francisco *Examiner* was read avidly throughout the West Coast. Bierce eventually retired and traveled to Mexico. Although a mystery surrounds his death, many believe he was killed during the siege of Ojinaga during the revolutionary turmoil of 1914.

The *Devil's Dictionary* (1906) includes numerous cynical definitions from his columns. His short stories are often compared to those of Poe for their elements of horror and of the supernatural. His best-known collection is *Can Such Things Be?* (1893). Bierce also published a 12-volume series, *Collected Works* (1909–1912).

BIERSTADT, ALBERT
1830–1902

Landscape painter, recognized for his immense, romantic canvases of the Rocky Mountain and Hudson River regions. German by birth, Bierstadt was raised in Massachusetts but returned to Europe to study art at the famed Dusseldorf Academy. There he learned the expansive painting

THE BANCROFT LIBRARY

Albert Bierstadt pours himself a drink in a double exposure taken by his brother.

style of the European Romantics. In 1858, he accompanied Frederick Landers on a survey party and laid eyes on the American West for the first time. The young artist was overwhelmed, and set out on his own to sketch the vast terrain. Bierstadt's immense canvases achieved greatest popularity during the 1860s and 1870s.

With the Civil War at an end, artists took in the vastness of the country in its entirety. Typical of the Rocky Mountain School, Bierstadt's canvases were enormous in size to reflect such images as the majestic, jutting peaks of the ROCKY MOUNTAINS, tall pines, and the vastness of the GRAND CANYON. His *Last of the Buffalo* (1888) warned of the vanishing of wildlife and of the Indians who depended on them.

Native Americans look on as Albert Bierstadt sketches in the Sierra Nevada.

Bierstadt's first Rocky Mountain pictures met with immediate success in 1860 at the National Academy of Design in New York City. The demand for his paintings in England soon made them the highest priced works of any American artist. But by the early 1880s, French Impressionism had gained public favor and relegated Bierstadt's panoramic views to a position of diminished prominence on the American art scene. Sales of his works declined, and he died in New York in 1902, almost forgotten by art critics and collectors. However, a peak in the Rocky Mountains was eventually named in his honor.

Two of his large canvases, *Discovery of the Hudson* and *Settlement of California,* hang in the Capitol in Washington, D.C.

BILLY THE KID
1859–1881

Born Henry McCarty, probably in New York City, he moved west with his widowed mother and ended up in New Mexico in 1873. When his mother remarried, he took his stepfather's name, Antrim. Later he adopted the alias of William H. Bonney. Usually he was known as Billy or the Kid.

The Kid's life of crime began in Silver City, New Mexico, when he was 15. After a brush with the law over a petty theft, he fled to Arizona. There, in a saloon fight on August 17, 1877, he shot and killed "Windy" Cahill, an older and bigger man who had bullied him.

The Kid fled to southeastern New Mexico, where became embroiled in the LINCOLN COUNTY WAR, a conflict between rival mercantile firms. Now 17, he signed on with the Tunstall–McSween "Regulators." In a series of gunfights with the Murphy–Dolan forces, he showed himself to be fearless and a crack shot. On April 1, 1878, he participated with five others in the ambush slaying in Lincoln of Sheriff William Brady. In

WESTERN AMERICANA PICTURE LIBRARY

Billy the Kid.

the final battle in the McSween House in Lincoln, on July 19, he led the breakout in which some of the defenders escaped.

In 1879–1880, based at old Fort Sumner in eastern New Mexico, Billy and a handful of comrades rustled cattle from stockmen in the nearby Texas Panhandle. He intended to go straight but never quite got around to it. In December 1880, following a shootout at Stinking Springs, Sheriff PAT GARRETT took him into custody. Convicted of the murder of Sheriff Brady and sentenced to be hanged, the Kid was held under guard in Lincoln. On April 28, 1881, he overpowered and killed his guard, fatally shot another deputy, and escaped. Newsmen now named him Billy the Kid.

Sheriff Garrett and his deputies tracked Billy to old Fort Sumner. There, on the night of July 14, 1881, Garrett accidentally confronted the fugitive in the darkened bedroom of one of the old military houses. Garrett fired twice, killing Billy instantly. The Kid was 21.

Fed by DIME NOVELS and later by motion pictures, a mighty legend took shape. Contrary to legend, however, Billy did not kill 21 men; he killed four on his own and participated in the killing of several more. He rustled cattle on a

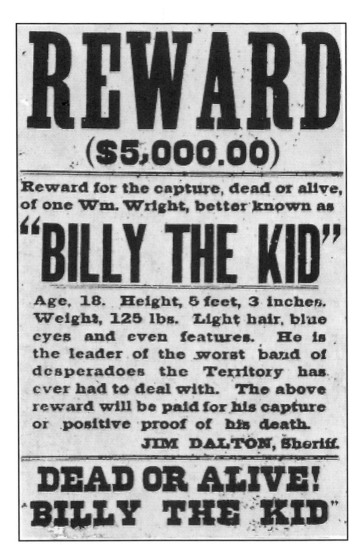

A notice advertising a reward for the capture of Billy the Kid.

minor scale, but he never robbed a bank or store or STAGE-COACH, or engaged in any other serious criminal activity. He was not the captain of an outlaw gang, nor was he a homicidal maniac. Instead, he was an intelligent, cheerful, and well-liked youth with a deadly temper. Despite the reality, Billy the Kid has become a legend cherished by people all over the world.

It did not take long for the life of Billy the Kid to become legend—this serial appeared the year of his death.

BINGHAM, GEORGE CALEB
1811–1879

In 1819 George Caleb Bingham's family moved from Virginia to central MISSOURI, the state that would remain his home for most of his life, that he celebrated with numerous paintings that richly present Missouri's social history, and that still retains the majority of his works. Bingham started to draw when quite young and remained largely self-taught. In 1827 he apprenticed to a cabinetmaker but, encouraged by the itinerant painter Chester Harding, he took up painting in earnest, producing work that was strong but crude in style. In 1837 he studied for three months at the Pennsylvania Academy of Fine Arts. After traveling to New York and then

George Caleb Bingham's painting Canvassing for a Vote, *depicting a campaigner soliciting votes.*

Philadelphia, Bingham settled down to portrait painting in Washington, D.C., from 1840 to 1844, after which he returned to Missouri. Aside from a later visit to Düsseldorf to study Germany's contemporary sentimental masters, he remained in Missouri. His paintings *Fur Traders Descending the Missouri* (1845), *Raftsmen Playing Cards* (1847), and *The Jolly Flatboatmen* (1846) evoke the era with strong geometrical compositions full of atmospheric light. Bingham's *Stump Speaking* (1854) explores a new subject matter, politics. After his Düsseldorf period (1856–1859) his work lost some of its luster, but he continued to paint.

Elected to the state legislature in 1848, as state treasurer in 1862, and as adjutant general in 1875, Bingham dallied with the prospect of a gubernatorial bid. In 1877 he became professor of art at the University of Missouri Columbia.

BLACK BART

See BOLES, CHARLES E.

BLACK ELK
1863–1950

A distant cousin of CRAZY HORSE, Black Elk was an Oglala SIOUX holy man. He was born near the Little Powder River in Wyoming, and as a teenager, he fought in the battle on the Little Big Horn River in which GEORGE ARMSTRONG CUSTER and his command were annihilated.

Following Crazy Horse's death at Fort Robinson, Nebraska, in 1877, Black Elk was taken by his family into Canada. After SITTING BULL's surrender at Fort Buford, Dakota Territory, in 1881, he and his family were placed on a South Dakota RESERVATION. In 1886 Black Elk joined WILLIAM F. "Buffalo Bill" CODY's Wild West show (as had Sitting Bull, a year earlier) and traveled with it in the United States and

Europe. He returned from a European tour in time to witness the tragedy at WOUNDED KNEE, on the Pine Ridge Reservation in South Dakota, in December 1890.

Black Elk was a lifelong mystic and visionary. His powers as a healer and his preaching on harmony with the changing world were celebrated not only among the Oglala but also among former white adversaries. In 1930 he was visited on the Pine Ridge Reservation by the poet John G. Neihardt, who interviewed him extensively, translated his memoirs, and published them as *Black Elk Speaks* in 1932. The book was praised by Carl Jung, among others, as an important contribution to world philosophy.

In 1947, at the age of 84, Black Elk, by then one of the few surviving Sioux to have firsthand knowledge of the religion and teachings of his tribe, agreed to have the Sioux ceremonies and thought recorded for posterity. Joseph E. Brown, an anthropologist, translated and wrote Black Elk's testimony on these subjects; the book was published in 1953 as *The Sacred Pipe*. Black Elk died on August 17, 1950.

BLACK HAWK WAR
Spring 1831–August 3, 1832

Led by Sauk war chief Black Hawk, one of the most implacable opponents of the white westward expansion, a group of approximately 300 Sauk (see IOWA) and Fox warriors, with women and children, crossed the MISSISSIPPI RIVER into Illinois in the spring of 1831. Their intent was to take up residence in Saukenuk, their traditional summer camp (present day Rock Island, Illinois). Confronted by a U.S. Army force of 1,500 men, the Indians withdrew across the river into Iowa.

Black Hawk returned the following spring, crossing the Mississippi on April 5, 1832, with a band now estimated at

Black Hawk (right) and his son, painted in 1833.

2,000 warriors, women, and children. A force of federal troops and state militia of equal strength, led by General Samuel Whiteside and Colonel ZACHARY TAYLOR, set out in pursuit a month later. A series of skirmishes ensued as Black Hawk's band slipped into Wisconsin. Other tribes, inspired by these successes, began to attack isolated settlements.

On June 15, President Andrew Jackson placed General WINFIELD SCOTT in command of the U.S. forces. Black Hawk proceeded west, planning to cross the Mississippi into Minnesota. His band, depleted by starvation and engagements with whites, had shrunk to about 500. On August 3, the federal troops, led by General Henry Atkinson, attacked near the confluence of the Mississippi and the Bad Axe. The resulting battle crushed Black Hawk's band and effectively ended his "war."

Besides Taylor and Scott, other future leaders who

served in the action war included Jefferson Davis and ABRAHAM LINCOLN.

BLACK HILLS

The Black Hills are a detached range of mountains whose peaks rise, on average, 4,000 feet above the prairie; they cover an area of 6,000 square miles in southwest South Dakota and northeastern WYOMING. Although the area was once the home of the ARAPAHOS, KIOWAS, and other tribes, it is most closely associated with the Lakota SIOUX.

Driven west by constant warfare with the OJIBWA, the Sioux, led by Standing Bull, probably reached the Black Hills (which they called *Paha Sapa*) around 1775. Certainly by the time LEWIS AND CLARK entered the region in 1803, the Sioux were firmly entrenched. The dark, wet, wooded hills stood in stark contrast to the dry grasslands below. Many Lakotas came to see Paha Sapa as sacred.

The FORT LARAMIE TREATY of April 29, 1868, included the Black Hills in the approximately 35,000 square miles set aside as part of the Great Sioux Reservation, despite rumors of GOLD in the mountains that began circulating as early as the 1850s. The treaty promised that the RESERVATION would be a permanent homeland for the Lakotas, but less than five years later white miners were encroaching on the Black Hills, prospecting for gold.

As demand for gold increased, however, the Army was ordered to make a reconnaissance of the area. In 1874, Lieutenant Colonel GEORGE ARMSTRONG CUSTER entered the Black Hills. His main mission was to scout a location for a fort, but he also took prospectors with him to look for gold. Upon returning, Custer said that gold had been found; he was reported as stating that the Hills were teeming with gold "from the grass roots down." Within a year, 11,000 prospectors had invaded. By 1876, 25,000 whites were in the area.

The U.S. government offered first to lease and then to buy the Black Hills from the Lakotas. Although many were adamantly opposed to any transaction, the tribe named a price of $70 million. When the federal commissioners offered only $6 million, negotiations broke down. The stage was set for the Battle of the LITTLE BIGHORN.

In the aftermath of the battle, in 1877 the Lakotas were forced to cede the Black Hills. Since then the Lakotas have been unceasing in their efforts to recover Paha Sapa. In 1980, the U.S. Supreme Court affirmed a judgment awarding the Indians over $100 million in damages. The Lakotas, however, refused the award, demanding instead the return of the area.

STATE HISTORICAL SOCIETY OF COLORADO

Black Kettle.

BLACK KETTLE
ca. 1810–1868

Black Kettle's age, parentage, and early life are disputed. By 1860, however, he was the leading peace chief of the Southern CHEYENNE. He was highly influential even though ridiculed by the war faction for his consistent willingness to accommodate the whites.

The Southern Cheyennes ranged the buffalo

Cheyenne Village Aug. 29th /64.

Maj. Colley.

Sir

We received a letter from Bent wishing us to make peace. We held a consel in regard to it all came to the conclusion to make peace with you providing you make peace with the Kiowas Commenches Arropahoes Apaches and Siouxs.

We are going to send a messenger to the Kiowas and to the other nations about our going to make with you. We heard that you some prisoners in Denver. We have seven prisoners of you which we are willing to give up providing you give up yours. There are three war parties out yet and two of Arrapohoes. they been out some time and expect now soon.

When we held this counsel there were few Arrapohoes and Siouxs present. we want true news from you in return, that is a letter

Black Kettle & other Chives

Brought t. McLym Sunday Sept 4th 1864 by One Eye

In one of his many attempts to reach a peaceful settlement with the whites, Black Kettle dictated this letter.

plains of Nebraska and Kansas. The SANTA FE, SMOKY HILL, and OREGON TRAILS cut across their homeland, and after the Civil War, railroads also began to encroach. In dealing with the Cheyennes, the federal government alternated diplomatic initiatives with military campaigns. Black Kettle invariably favored the treaty over the warpath, and he opposed the chiefs who believed war to be the only solution to the rising white threat. His mark headed the list of chiefs who signed the Fort Wise Treaty of 1861, by which the Cheyennes yielded all their lands in exchange for a small RESERVATION south of the Arkansas River. The war chiefs, however, refused to sign, and the Indian War of 1864 resulted.

Black Kettle sought to end the war by negotiating with government officials. At a conference at Camp Weld, near Denver, he was told to take his people to Fort Lyon and surrender. At Fort Lyon, however, the military authorities instructed him to remain in camp on Sand Creek. In truth, Black Kettle's initiative interfered with plans to punish the Indians for summer raids on the travel routes to Denver, and to force them to vacate the lands supposedly yielded at Fort Wise. Black Kettle thought he was at peace, but at dawn on November 29, 1864, Colonel JOHN M. CHIVINGTON and a cavalry force attacked the village and perpetrated the infamous SAND CREEK MASSACRE, which took the lives of more than 100 people, most of them women and children.

In retaliation for Sand Creek, the Cheyenne war groups joined with the SIOUX to ravage the Plains settlements and travel routes, then withdrew far to the north. Black Kettle and the peace elements remained in the south. In October 1867, with chiefs of the KIOWAS and COMANCHES, he again met with government emissaries and signed the MEDICINE LODGE TREATY. Like the Fort Wise Treaty, this document bound the Cheyennes to relinquish the Central Plains and settle on reservations to the south, in the Indian Territory.

Although Black Kettle took his own people south, other Cheyenne bands remained in their traditional areas. War erupted again in 1868. Black Kettle tried to stay out of it, but he could not control his young men. A raiding party left a trail in the snow that led to his village on the Washita River. At dawn on November 27, 1868, a military column under Lieutenant Colonel GEORGE ARMSTRONG CUSTER launched a surprise attack. In the first charge, Black Kettle and his wife, seeking to escape, were cut down and fell dead in the icy waters of the river.

BLACKFEET

The Blackfeet are a group of Algonquian Native American tribes of the Northern Plains and Canada. They are often confused with the Lakota SIOUX tribe that is also named Blackfeet.

Bear Bull, Blackfoot medicine man.

The group is composed of the Piegan (or Pikuni), Blood (or Kainah), and the Blackfeet proper (or Siksika). These are separate tribes with a common language but their own organizations. In addition, the GROS VENTRE (or Atsina), a division of the ARAPAHOS, and the Sarsi, an ATHAPASKAN-speaking tribe, are closely associated with the Blackfeet and are often erroneously referred to as Blackfeet. The Blackfeet may have migrated from the Northeast. When first encountered by whites in the eighteenth century, they were one of the most powerful groups of Native Americans on the Plains, holding a vast territory east of the Rockies in the United States and Canada. They were at continual war with their neighbors, including the Shoshones, Crees, Arapahos, and CROWS.

After the Blackfeet became active in the FUR TRADE, they came into more conflict with other tribes, including the FLAT-HEADS. Sometimes the Blackfeet raided the territory of other tribes in order to secure their own borders and to take BUF-FALO. They also allowed both the British to establish trading

The Blackfeet, *painted by Alfred Jacob Miller.*

A peace meeting between the Blackfeet and the Nez Perce and Flathead tribes in 1855, painted by Gustavus Sohon.

Nomadic Canadian Blackfeet Indians lived in buffalo-hide lodges in temporary villages.

companies and the United States to set up outposts in their domain. They seem to have reached the height of their power around 1830, with an estimated population of between 10,000 and 18,000 in their territory. But the 1836 smallpox

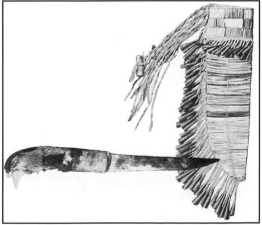

The Blackfeet made their own knives and sheaths.

Blackfoot tipis, painted by William Armstrong.

epidemic wiped out half their people, and some villages lost as many as three-quarters of their population.

Although in some ways the fur trade helped the Blackfeet to secure their territory against other Native Americans, it did nothing to affect the demand for land by white settlers. In 1855, in a treaty with the United States that also permitted the building of U.S. roads and forts, Blackfeet territory was defined. The Blackfeet, in exchange, were to receive $20,000 per year for ten years, plus schools, missions, health care, various goods, and protection of their territorial integrity. Most of these promises were not kept.

The Blackfeet were aggressive in the defense of their own lands against other tribes, as well as the United States or Canada. During the campaigns to push all northern tribes onto RESERVATIONS, U.S. cavalry attacked a peaceful Piegan village on the Marias River in MONTANA in January 1870. Of the 173 Indians killed, 140 were women and children, 18 were old men, and only 15 were warriors.

BODMER, KARL
1809–1893

A Swiss draftsman, painter, and etcher whose detailed work provides valuable documentary about Native Americans and landscapes of the American West, Karl Bodmer was selected by Prince Maximilian of Wied, a small German principality, to tour and document scenes of North America in 1832. The prince wanted Bodmer's drawings in order to increase European knowledge of the Native American inhabitants, who had received very little attention. Bodmer studied the paintings of GEORGE CATLIN and Samuel Seymour to prepare for the two-year assignment. Maximillian and Bod-

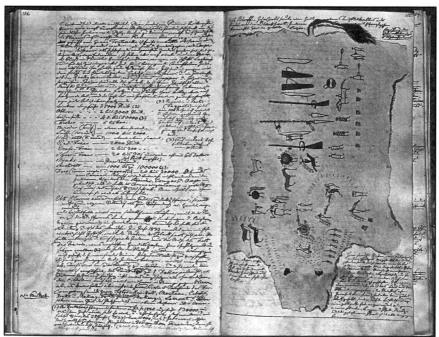

This section of Prince Maximilians' 1834 journal includes Bodmer's illustration (right), of an Indian buffalo hide. The Indians recorded their battles on such skins.

Karl Bodmer's portrait of Pehriska-Ruhpa, a Moennitarri warrior, in a Dog Dance costume.

mer set out from St. Louis, Missouri, aboard the AMERICAN FUR COMPANY steamer, the *Yellowstone,* and traveled up the MISSOURI RIVER. Bodmer sketched Indians at every opportunity, often taking an entire day to create a single watercolor portrait. He worked meticulously, sketching the jewelry and costumes in great detail. In 1834 Bodmer returned to Europe and worked his sketches into colored engravings for the atlas of Maximilian's work, *Travels.* Bodmer resided in France until his death in 1893. The 427 original watercolors created during the expedition were discovered at Neuweid castle after World War II and are displayed at the Joslyn Art Museum in Omaha, Nebraska.

LIBRARY OF CONGRESS

Charles E. Boles.

BOLES, CHARLES E.
ca. 1830–ca. 1917

Little is known of Boles (who also used the named Charles E. Bolton) a CALIFORNIA STAGECOACH robber known as Black Bart, other than his exploits against WELLS FARGO during the period 1875–1883. He appears to have been a New Yorker who had come West as a young man, perhaps as a Forty-niner, and had served in the Civil War. In all, he robbed 28 stagecoaches of their strongboxes (he never robbed passengers) in northern California. He wore a linen duster and a flour-sack mask, and carried an unloaded shotgun. Twice he left good-natured verses behind, signed "Black Bart, the Po-8."

After a botched robbery in which he was slightly wounded, Boles was tracked down by a Wells Fargo detective. In November 1883 he pleaded guilty and was sentenced to six years in San Quentin penitentiary. After serving four years, he disappeared. A New York newspaper carried his obituary in 1917.

BOLEY, OKLAHOMA

One of several all-black western towns that sprang up at the turn of the century, Boley brought hope to AFRICAN-AMERICANS fleeing discrimination and seeking new opportunities.

After the CIVIL WAR, many African-Americans hoped to obtain property and begin forging new lives. But in the South, many were unable to get the kind of land they wanted and needed. Since the government was actively pushing settlement west of the MISSISSIPPI, many African-Americans looked there for relief from discrimination.

It was announced that blacks had the same rights as other citizens to preempt or take homesteads. Further, BEN-JAMIN "PAP" SINGLETON and others spread news of greater economic opportunity and political freedom in KANSAS and its border states. Such promise caused a great exodus of blacks westward during the 1870s and 1880s, and the "EXODUSTER" movement reached its peak in 1879.

Of the 25 black communities formed in OKLAHOMA between 1890 and 1910, Boley became the largest and best known. It sprang up in response to African-Americans' increasing exclusion from white communities in the surrounding Indian Territory.

Lake Moore, an executive of the Fort Smith and Western Railroad Townsite Company, was impressed with his black employees and proposed building a RAILROAD town that could become the nucleus of an all-black community. They bought land in Okfuskee County, part of Oklahoma's Indian Territory, where many blacks had been given land grants. Moore's boss, B. T. Boley, supported the idea and gave the town its name in 1903.

Settlers soon flocked to the site, spurred by stories of fertile, unoccupied land. Many were Texas sharecroppers seeking independence. Boley's town fathers advertised in black newspapers around the nation, including their own *Boley Progress*. Booker T. Washington and other prominent citizens praised it as a place where African-Americans could find financial success and racial dignity.

Located in a fertile farm belt, Boley encompassed 80 acres and had more than 40,000 residents. In 1903, the first black post office and postmaster were authorized. Within a short time, the flourishing community boasted two banks, two cotton mills, a hotel, and the tallest building between Oklahoma City and Okmulgee. More importantly, it celebrated the fact that half of its high school students entered college, which for many was Boley's Creek Seminole College and Agricultural Institute. African-Americans ran the government, making it influential among similar settlements.

But outside influences and discrimination stunted Boley's growth. The Western Negro Press Association asked President THEODORE ROOSEVELT not to admit Oklahoma into the Union until the government assured that it would not pass laws discriminating against blacks. But Roosevelt never responded, and when Oklahoma finally entered the Union in 1907, Congress, too, declined to make such demands. The final blow to hopes for racial equality occurred in 1910 when Oklahoma enacted a grandfather clause. This disenfranchised its black citizens on the basis that their grandfathers, as slaves, had not voted. Racial violence forced many blacks out of nearby settlements, and the dream of independence and self-rule in Oklahoma was destroyed.

BONANZA FARMS

Bonanza farms were expansive farms that flourished in the 1880s in the wheat fields of the north central prairies and plains. The bonanza farms thrived on the components of industrial capitalism—the application of machinery to mass production, absentee ownership, professional management, specialization, and cheap labor. These sprawling enterprises not only imitated the railroads' corporate design, but were also often formed on former RAILROAD land.

After the Panic of 1873, the NORTHERN PACIFIC RAILROAD went bankrupt. Bondholders could turn in their greatly depreciated bonds to obtain portions of its 50 million acres of land in MINNESOTA and North Dakota. The value for the land at the time was a mere $.37 to $1.65 per acre. Many investors, including the president of the Northern Pacific, George W. Cass, recognized the tremendous opportunity for acquiring huge tracts of land cheaply and had the necessary capital. Those who could purchase over 3,000 acres held title to what would be termed a "bonanza."

Cass and Benjamin Cheney, a director of the Northern Pacific, bought almost 13,500 acres near Casselton, North Dakota, paying about $.40 to $.60 per acre. Almost 90 such great land tracts were bought. They ranged between 15,000 and 50,000 acres. New developments in machinery and milling processes, together with the flat and fertile prairie land, high demand for wheat, and readily available labor force fueled these bonanza farm enterprises.

Most owners, such as the Amenia and Sharon Land Company of Sharon, Connecticut, hired managers and ruled the Red River Valley farms in absentia. Under the managers, the farms were divided and overseen using a professional management system of superintendents, each of whom oversaw several foremen. The mass labor force was often migrant, since fewer hands were needed during seeding and threshing seasons than during plowing and haying seasons.

The enormous scale of the farms attracted national attention, and drew an inrush of settlers to the region. The hired men came from nearby homesteads, cities, and lumber camps and usually worked a 13-hour day for wages of $16 to $25 a month with room and board.

Many bonanza owners had assumed that such an operation would be temporary, yet some farms lasted for several years. Rising land taxes and the increasing value of the land, however, caused the dissolution of many bonanza farms with an almost guaranteed profit to the owners.

BONNEY, WILLIAM

See BILLY THE KID

BOOMERS

In the eighteenth and nineteenth centuries, the term "boomers" was applied to migrants who moved illegally into land that had not been settled by non-Native Americans and that usually was owned by the federal government. The first example of such a squatter colony goes back to the 1760s, when settlers moved into areas as far-flung as the Old Northwest and West Florida in defiance of the Proclamation of 1763. A more spectacular example dates to 1875–1876, when some 15,000 miners invaded the BLACK HILLS in search of GOLD.

The term achieved its greatest currency in OKLAHOMA, where boomers, led by ex-soldier David Payne, invaded lands owned by members of the FIVE CIVILIZED TRIBES. In spite of numerous arrests and forced removals by the U.S. Army, the boomers kept returning. Payne claimed that the lands had been owned by the Indians under the treaties they had signed with the United States in 1866 and therefore were covered under the HOMESTEAD ACT. Payne would continue to battle with U.S. authorities until his death in 1884. The movement he led undoubtedly hastened the opening of the Indian and Oklahoma Territories to white settlers.

BOONE, DANIEL
1734–1820

The son of Quakers, Boone learned the rudiments of reading and writing, helped the family by farming and black-smithing, and showed a keen talent for hunting and trapping. The family moved to North Carolina in 1750, and Daniel accompanied the Braddock Expedition to Fort Duquesne in 1755. He married Rebecca Bryan in 1756 but did not settle down to traditional domesticity. Although not the first explorer or discoverer of Kentucky, as legend has it, Boone entered Kentucky in 1767, and again in 1769, when he began a hunt that lasted two years, and traded with the Shawnee Indians. In 1773, while he was leading several families to settle in Kentucky, his party was attacked by Cherokees; his son James was captured, tortured, and murdered.

Richard Henderson of the Transylvania Company hired Boone in March 1775 to blaze Boone's Trace, or the Wilderness Road, from Cumberland Gap, Virginia, to the Kentucky River; by September he had brought his wife and daughter to the fort and settlement of Boonesborough on the Kentucky River. As a captain in the county militia, he staved off Indian attacks on Boonesborough, but in 1778 he was captured by the Shawnee. He cooperated with them—their chief, Black-fish, adopted Boone as his son, calling him "Big Turtle." After five months Boone escaped and raced to warn the Boonesborough residents of an imminent attack by a joint force of

British soldiers and Shawnees. Instrumental in the successful defense against a ten-day siege, Boone was promoted to major. The preservation of the fort proved vital to continued westward migration and settlement.

During the Revolutionary War, Boone served in Fayette County as lieutenant colonel of the militia, legislator, county lieutenant, and deputy surveyor. In 1781 he was captured in Charlottesville, Virginia, by the British under Colonel Banastre Tarleton and released after several days. In 1782

Daniel Boone.

he saw action at Bryan's Station and the Battle of Blue Licks. After the war Boone moved farther west, seeking less settled areas. He served as a legislator in present-day West Virginia; in 1799 he and his family joined his son Daniel Morgan Boone in Missouri, where he continued to hunt and trap and served as a magistrate.

Boone's continued failure to establish land claims and his indomitable wanderlust kept him moving about. He sold a land grant from the U.S. Congress in 1815 to pay off debts. He died in 1820 but was not forgotten; in 1823 Lord Byron immortalized the backwoods pioneer in buckskin in his poem *Don Juan:*

G. SHOMAEKERS ARCHIVE

"Boonesborough" was founded by Boone in 1775.

Of all men, saving Sylla the man-slayer
Who passes for in life and death most lucky,
Of the great names which in our faces stare,
The General Boon, back-woodsman of Kentucky,
Was happiest amongst mortals anywhere;
For killing nothing but a bear or buck, he
Enjoy'd the lonely, vigorous, harmless days
Of his old age in wilds of deepest maze.

(Canto VIII, stanza 61)

LIBRARY OF CONGRESS

Gutzon Borglum.

BORGLUM, GUTZON
1871–1941

John Gutzon de la Mothe Borglum (born in Idaho Territory, March 25, 1871) was a sculptor famous for his Mount Rushmore (BLACK HILLS, South Dakota) carving of the heads of four U.S. presidents.

He ran away from his Danish Mormon parents at the age of 12 and settled in San Francisco, where he learned lithography and fresco painting through brief apprenticeships. Two years later he moved to Los Angeles and began to amass a portfolio of work, primarily of western subjects. In 1888 Borglum gave away many of these paintings to repay the benefactors who supported his further study in Paris. In 1895 he exhibited his early works (including *Indian Scouts, Death of a Chief,* and *Apaches Pursued by U.S. Troops*) in New York, London, and Paris. He returned to New York in 1901 to concentrate on sculpting horses, the main subject for the work of his older brother SOLON HANNI-BAL BORGLUM, also a sculptor.

Borglum's interest soon turned to large-scale sculpture, primarily in the form of public monuments. His most important commissions include the head of Abraham Lincoln in the rotunda of the Capitol in Washington, D.C., and a commemoration of the Wars of America in Newark, New Jersey. (A large-scale memorial to the Confederate Army was begun in 1916 at Stone Mountain near Atlanta, Georgia, but the project was stalled by controversy and left unfinished.)

In 1927, applying special techniques such as the controlled use of dynamite, Borglum began the project at Mount Rushmore. The heads of U.S. presidents George Washington, Thomas Jefferson, Theodore Roosevelt, and Abraham Lincoln were sculpted out of the mountain. He died on March 6, 1941, and his son, Lincoln, finished the project.

LIBRARY OF CONGRESS

Solon Hannibal Borglum.

BORGLUM, SOLON HANNIBAL
1868–1922

This sculptor's lively horses and Indian figures capture the spirit of the Old West.

Born in 1868 in Ogden, Utah, of Danish Mormon parents, Solon Borglum grew up on the prairies of Nebraska. His early years as a ranchhand influenced the young artist's choice of subjects for sketching. At the age of 25, he set out for

California to pursue his passion for art. He joined his younger brother, GUTZON BORGLUM, at a studio in the Sierra Madre. Borglum exhibited locally but left California in 1895 to study with Louis Rebisso, head instructor of sculpture at the Cincinnati Academy of Art. There the artist dissected horses and attended human surgical clinics to immerse himself in details of anatomy.

Later, as a student at the Académie Julien in Paris, his horse sculptures (*Lassoing Wild Horses, Stampede of Wild Horses,* and *The Lame Horse*) won salon awards and wide acclaim. But it was not until 1899, during an extended visit to the Crow Creek Reservation in South Dakota, that Borglum gained access to Indian models and, through them, enhanced his knowledge of Native American customs and traditions. At "Rocky Ranch" in Silvermine, Connecticut, he continued to create dynamic bronze figures and bucking broncos, until service in World War I interrupted his work. Upon his release, Borglum founded the School of American Sculpture in New York, and acted as its director until his death in 1922.

His work includes important civic sculptures at Prescott, Arizona; Atlanta, Georgia; and New Rochelle, New York. Although his reputation was overshadowed by that of his brother, Gutzon, who carved the immense presidential heads into Mount Rushmore, Solon's bronze sculptures and lifesize monuments offer an animated representation of the spirit of the Old West.

LIBRARY OF CONGRESS

Elias Boudinot.

BOUDINOT, ELIAS
1803–1839

Boudinot, a noted Cherokee writer and political figure, was the editor of the first Indian newspaper. He was born Buck Watie (or Gallegina) but changed his name to Elias Boudinot in honor of his mentor of the same name, a former president of the Continental Congress and the president of the American Bible Society.

Educated at the Foreign Mission School in Cornwall, Connecticut, Boudinot early on became a proponent of Christianity and Indian assimilation. He is sometimes credited with being the first Native-American novelist, as the author of *Poor Sarah, or Religion Exemplified in the Life and Death of an Indian Woman,* probably written in 1823. The work, however, little more than a proselytizing pamphlet, is generally considered to have been copied from non-Indian sources. Later, Boudinot helped Samuel Worcester translate the Bible into Cherokee.

From 1824 to 1835 he served as the editor of the *Cherokee Phoenix.* Published in both English and Cherokee, it was the first Indian newspaper in the country. By the early 1830s, Boudinot, along with his cousin JOHN RIDGE and other influential Cherokees, became convinced that removal to the West was inevitable. He became a leading figure of the so-called Treaty Party, which advocated negotiation with the United States concerning removal. In 1835, he was a key figure in the negotiation of the Treaty of New Echota, which led to the infamous TRAIL OF TEARS. Upon moving to Indian Territory, Boudinot was considered a traitor by those who opposed removal. In 1839, he was ambushed and executed by members of the Cherokee Nation loyal to Principal Chief JOHN ROSS.

GLOSSARY

Adobe A building material consisting of sun-dried bricks made from a mixture of clay and straw. (See article.)

Alta California A former Spanish and Mexican province that now comprises the state of California. (See Baja California.)

Antebellum period The period of American history preceding the Civil War.

Anti-coolie associations Organizations formed in California in the late 1860s to attack Chinese workers and discourage factories from employing such workers.

Artillery Large-caliber weapons, such as cannon, operated by crews.

Baja California The lower portion of the former Spanish province of California that now comprises the Mexican states of Baja California and Baja California Sur. It is a peninsula south of the U.S. state of California.

Barbed wire Fencing made of twisted strands of wire with barbs at regular intervals; first patented by Joseph H. Glidden. (See article.)

Bauxite Aluminum ore; composed mainly of hydrous aluminum oxides and aluminum hydroxides.

Beaver A member of the rodent family with a long flat tail; prized by trappers and furriers for its pelt. (See article.)

Bison A bovine mammal of western North America characterized by a large head and forequarters, short curved horns, and a shaggy mane; commonly referred to as a buffalo.

Bowie knife A single-edged steel hunting knife, 10 to 15 inches long, with a horn handle and a curved tip; attributed to Jim Bowie but probably designed by his brother Rezin.

Buffalo *See* bison.

Buffalo soldiers Black soldiers of the United States regular army who fought Indians and policed the western frontier in the decades following the Civil War; so named for their thickly curled hair.

Camas A plant in the lily family with blue flowers and an edible bulb; an important part of the diet of the Bannock tribe. (See article.)

Cavalry An army unit composed of mounted soldiers trained to fight on horseback.

Claim A tract of public land claimed through formal procedures by a miner or homesteader.

Claim jumper An individual who steals a mining claim by forcing the owner to flee.

Confluence The point at which two streams or rivers meet.

Conquistador One of the sixteenth-century Spanish soldiers who defeated the civilizations of the New World; a conqueror.

Coolie Slang term for an unskilled Asian laborer; usually carried a negative connotation.

Cowboy A herdsman who tends cattle, usually on horseback; responsible for keeping the cattle together, guiding them to pasture, protecting them from rustlers, branding them, and driving them to the shipping point. (See article.)

Desperado A bold or desperate outlaw.

Dime novel A melodramatic novel of romance or adventure; named for the Dime Book Series published by Erastus Beadle. (See article.)

Emancipation Liberation from bondage, as in the freeing of all slaves in the United States after the Civil War.

Ethnology The analysis and comparison of human cultures; cultural anthropology.

Forty-niners Prospectors who came to California to stake claims after gold was discovered there in 1849; see California Gold Rush.

Gold rush An influx of a large number of prospectors into an area following the discovery of a rich deposit of gold.

Grandfather clause A clause in the constitutions of several southern states before 1915 whose purpose was to prevent blacks from voting; such clauses established strict voting requirements that did not have to be met by the lineal descendants of individuals who had registered to vote before 1867. Also used in a broader sense in other legal documents.

Great Plains The grassland plateau of central North America stretching east from the base of the Rocky Mountains.

Guerrilla A member of an irregular military unit operating in small bands to undermine an enemy.

Gulch A small ravine.

Homesteader A person who claims and settles land.

Indian removal The policy of moving Indian tribes from the eastern United States to lands in the West that were not inhabited by whites or included within the boundries of any state; the primary Indian policy during the 1830s and 1840s.

Infantry An army unit composed of soldiers trained to fight on foot, chiefly with small arms.

Irregular A soldier who is not part of an established military force.

Jim Crow A set of laws and practices that systematically discriminated against blacks in the southern states from the late 1860s to the early 1970s.

Longhorn A breed of cattle of Spanish origin characterized by long horns; the most popular type of cattle in Texas during the early years of the cattle business.

Lunette A fortification jutting out from a wall that can serve as a cannon emplacement.

Magazine A place where ammunition and explosives are stored.

Mesa A broad, flat-topped elevation with one or more cliff-like sides; common in the southwestern United States.

Militia A military force that is not part of a regular army and may be called up in times of emergency.

Mission A group of persons sent to a foreign country by a religious organization to spread its faith; also the building or compound in which those persons are housed.

Mormon A member of the Church of Jesus Christ of Latter-day Saints, founded by Joseph Smith in 1830 and headquartered since 1847 in Salt Lake City, Utah. (See article.)

Musket A shoulder gun used in the seventeenth and eighteenth centuries.

Nugget A small, solid lump, especially of gold.

Ordnance Military equipment, weapons, and ammunition.

Parapet A low protective wall along the edge of a raised structure.

Pike A long spear formerly used by infantry.

Placer deposit A glacial or alluvial deposit of sand or gravel that contains eroded particles of a valuable mineral such as gold.

Plain A very large, treeless area of flat or rolling country.

Plateau An elevated, relatively level expanse of land.

Prairie An extensive area of flat or rolling grassland.

Presidio A fort of the kind established by the Spanish to protect their holdings and missions in the southwestern United States.

Prospector A person who explores an area in search of mineral deposits or oil.

Pueblo A village consisting of multilevel, terraced adobe or stone apartment dwellings around a central plaza; the typical community of the Pueblo peoples of New Mexico and Arizona.

Quarantine A period of enforced isolation of people or animals suspected of carrying a contagious disease, imposed to prevent the spread of the disease.

Rancho An extensive farm on which large herds of cattle, sheep, or horses are raised; a ranch. (See article.)

Reconstruction The period from 1865 to 1877, during which the federal government ruled the Confederate states before readmitting them fully to the Union.

Rendezvous The annual meeting of fur trappers, at which they disposed of the year's catch, received the next year's supplies, and rested.

Repeating rifle a rifle that can be fired several times without being reloaded.

Reservation A tract of land set apart by the federal government for a particular Native American people. (See article.)

Rodeo A competition or exhibition in which skills related to cattle ranching, such as roping calves, are displayed.

Rustling Stealing livestock, especially cattle.

Sapper A military engineer who specializes in fortification and related activities.

Sectional controversy The conflict between northern and southern states in the period before the Civil War.

Sharecropper A tenant farmer who gives a share of the crops to the landlord in place of rent.

Stagecoach A four-wheeled, horse-drawn vehicle used to transport passengers and mail over a regular route.

Texas fever An infectious disease of cattle characterized by high fever, anemia, and emaciation; first identified in Texas.

Texas Panhandle The narrow strip of territory projecting northward from central Texas.

Texas Rangers A special law enforcement corps in the State of Texas, first organized in 1835 and still in existence; an emergency force for situations beyond the control of local police or a sheriff.

Trading post A store in a sparsely settled area where supplies are traded for local products.

Viceroy A person who governs a country, province, or colony as the representative of a monarch.

Vigilance committee A group formed to carry out unauthorized law enforcement activities.

Vigilante A person who engages in unauthorized law enforcement activities or is a member of a group engaging in such activities.

FURTHER READINGS

ANDERSON, NANCY K. *Albert Bierstadt: Art and Enterprise.* New York: Hudson Hills Press, 1990.

ANDRIST, RALPH K. *The Long Death: The Last Days of the Plains Indian.* New York: Macmillan, 1964.

BAIGELL, MATTHEW. *Albert Bierstadt.* New York: Watson-Guptill, 1981.

BAKELESS, JOHN EDWIN. *Daniel Boone.* New York: W. Morrow, 1939.

BALL, LARRY D. *Elfego Baca in Life and Legend.* El Paso, TX: Texas Western Press, 1992.

BEACHUM, LARRY M. *William Becknell: Father of the Santa Fe Trade.* El Paso, TX: Texas Western Press, 1982.

BECKETT, V.B. *Baca's Battle.* Houston: Stagecoach Press, 1962.

BENEDEK, EMILY. *The Wind Won't Know Me: A History of the Navajo-Hopi Land Dispute.* New York: Knopf, 1992.

BERNARD, JACQUELINE. *Voices from the Southwest: Antonio Jose Martinez, Elfego Baca, Reies Lopez Tijerina.* New York: Scholastic Book Services, 1972.

BILLINGTON, RAY ALLEN. *Land of Savagery/Land of Promise: The European Image of the American Frontier in the Nineteenth Century.* New York: Norton, 1981.

BOWMAN, JOHN S., ed. *The World Almanac of the American West.* Introduction by Alvin M. Josephy, Jr. New York: Ballantine Books, 1986.

BREIHAN, CARL W. *Great Gunfighters of the West.* San Antonio, TX: Naylor, 1971.

BROWN, DEE. *Bury My Heart at Wounded Knee: An Indian History of the American West.* New York: Henry Holt, 1970.

BUTTERFIELD, ROGER. *The American Past: A History of the United States from Concord to the Great Society*. New York: Simon and Schuster, 1976.

CAPTURE, GEORGE HORSE, ed. *The Seven Visions of Bull Lodge*. Ann Arbor, MI: Bear Claw Press, 1980.

CARMODY, DENISE LARDNER, and JOHN TULLY. *Native American Religions: An Introduction*. New York: Paulist Press, 1993.

CARPENTER, ALLAN. *The Encyclopedia of the Far West*. New York: Facts on File, 1991.

CARROLL, JOHN M., ed. *The Black Military Experience in the American West*. New York: Liveright Publishing, 1971.

CHRISMAN, HARRY E. *The 1,001 Most Asked Questions about the American West*. Chicago: Swallow Press, 1982.

CHRIST-JANER, ALBERT. *George Caleb Bingham: Frontier Painter of Missouri*. New York: H.N. Abrams, 1975.

CLINE, DONALD. *Alias Billy the Kid: The Man Behind the Legend*. Santa Fe, NM: Sunstone Press, 1986.

COMSTOCK, ESTHER J. *Feliciana's California Miracle*. Grass Valley, CA: Comstock Bonanza Press, 1985.

CONLEY, ROBERT J. *Geronimo: An American Legend*. New York: Pocket Books, 1994.

CORTESI, LAWRENCE. *Jim Beckwourth: Explorer-Patriot of the Rockies*. New York: Criterion Books, 1971.

CROMIE, ALICE. *Tour Guide to the Old West*. New York: Quadrangle/New York Times Book Company, 1977.

DAVIES, ALFRED MERVYN. *Solon H. Borglum: "A Man Who Stands Alone."* Chester, CT: Pequot Press, 1974.

DAVIS, MARY, ed. *Native America in the Twentieth Century*. New York: Garland, 1994.

DE CASTRO, ADOLPHE DANZIGER. *Portrait of Ambrose Bierce*. New York: Beekman Publishers, 1974.

DILLON, RICHARD H. *Humbugs and Heroes: A Gallery of California Pioneers*. Garden City, NY: Doubleday, 1970.

ELMAN, ROBERT. *Badmen of the West*. Secaucus, NJ: Castle Books, 1974.

EWERS, JOHN CANFIELD. *Artists of the Old West.* Garden City, NY: Doubleday, 1973.

FARAGHER, JOHN MACK. *Daniel Boone: The Life and Legend of an American Pioneer.* New York: Holt, 1992.

FEHRENBACH, T.R. *Lone Star: A History of Texas and The Texans.* New York: Macmillan, 1968.

FEJES, CLAIRE. *Villagers: Athabaskan Indian Life along the Yukon River.* New York: Random House, 1981.

FIREMAN, BERT M. *Arizona: Historic Land.* Foreword by Lawrence Clark Powell. New York: Knopf, 1982.

FOWLER, LORETTA. *The Arapaho.* Edited by Frank W. Porter II. New York: Chelsea House, 1989.

FRAZIER, IAN. *Great Plains.* New York: Farrar Straus Giroux, 1989.

FREDRICKSON, GEORGE M. *The Black Image in the White Mind: The Debate on Afro-American Character and Destiny, 1817–1914.* New York: Harper & Row, 1971.

GETCHES, DAVID H. *Cases and Materials on Federal Indian Law.* St. Paul, MN: West Publishing, 1986.

GETCHES, DAVID H., et al. *Federal Indian Law.* St. Paul, MN: West Publishing, 1993.

GOWANS, FRED R. *Rocky Mountain Rendezvous: A History of the Fur Trade Rendezvous, 1825–1840.* Salt Lake City: Peregrine Smith Books, 1985.

HAMMOND, GEORGE PETER. *The Adventures of Alexander Barclay.* Denver: Old West Publishing, 1976.

HASSRICK, PETER H. *Artists of the American Frontier: The Way West.* New York: Promontory Press, 1988.

HENDRICKS, GORDON. *Albert Bierstadt: Painter of the American West.* New York: Harry N. Abrams, 1974.

HINCKLEY, TED C. *The Americanization of Alaska: 1867–1897.* Palo Alto, CA: Pacific Books, 1972.

HOIG, STAN. *The Battle of Washita: The Sheridan-Custer Indian Campaign of 1867–69.* Garden City, NY: Doubleday, 1976.

———. *The Cheyenne.* New York: Chelsea House, 1989.

HORAN, JAMES D. *The Outlaws: The Authentic Wild West.* New York: Crown, 1977.

HUNGRY WOLF, ADOLF. *The Blood People: A Division of the Blackfoot Confederacy*. New York: Harper & Row, 1977.

HYDE, DAYTON O. *The Last Free Man: The True Story Behind the Massacre of Shoshone Mike and His Band of Indians in 1911*. New York: Dial Press, 1973.

INMAN, HENRY. *The Old Santa Fe Trail: The Story of a Great Highway*. Minneapolis: Ross & Haines, 1966.

INNIS, BEN. *Bloody Knife: Custer's Favorite Scout*. Fort Collins, CO: Old Army Press, 1973.

IRVING, WASHINGTON. *Astoria: Anecdotes of an Enterprise Beyond the Rocky Mountains*. Edited by Richard Dilworth Rust. Boston: Twayne Publishers, 1976.

JACOBS, DONALD M. *Antebellum Black Newspapers*. Westport, CT: Greenwood Press, 1976.

JAIMES, M. ANNETTE, ed. *The State of Native America*. Boston: South End Press, 1992.

JONES, JOAN MEGAN. *The Art and Style of Western Indian Basketry*. Blaine, WA: Hancock House, 1982.

JOSEPHY, ALVIN M., JR., ed. *The American Heritage Book of Indians*. New York: American Heritage Publishing, 1961.

———, ed. *The American Heritage History of the Great West*. New York: American Heritage Publishing, 1965.

———. *The Patriot Chiefs*. New York: Viking, 1961.

KATZ, WILLIAM LOREN. *Black Indians: A Hidden Heritage*. New York: Atheneum, 1986.

———. *The Black West*. Seattle: Open Hand, 1987.

LAMAR, HOWARD R., ed. *The Reader's Encyclopedia of the American West*. New York: Thomas Y. Crowell, 1977.

LAZARUS, EDWARD. *Black Hills/White Justice*. New York: Harper-Collins, 1991.

LONG, JEFF. *Duel of Eagles: The Mexican and U.S. Fight for the Alamo*. New York: Morrow, 1990.

MAY, ROBIN. *Gunfighters*. New York: Gallery Books, 1984.

MCCRACKEN, HAROLD. *Great Painters of the Old West*. New York: Dover, 1988.

MELODY, MICHAEL EDWARD. *The Apache*. New York: Chelsea House, 1989.

METZ, LEON CLAIRE. *Border: The U.S.- Mexico Line*. El Paso, TX: Mangan Books, 1989.

———. *The Shooters*. El Paso, TX: Mangan Books, 1976.

MORGAN, DALE L. *The West of William H. Ashley: 1822–1838*. Denver: Old West Publishing, 1964.

NATION, DENE. *Denedeh: A Dene Celebration*. Yellowknife, N.W.T.: Dene Nation, 1984.

NEVIN, DAVID. *The Texans*. New York: Time-Life Books, 1975.

NICHOLS, ROGER L. *Black Hawk and the Warrior's Path*. Arlington Heights, IL: Harlan Davidson, 1992.

OLEKSA, MICHAEL, ed. *Alaskan Spirituality*. New York: Paulist Press, 1987.

PORTER, KENNETH WIGGINS. *The Negro on the American Frontier*. Preface by William Loren Katz. New York: Arno Press, 1971.

POURADE, RICHARD F. *Anza Conquers the Desert: The Anza Expeditions from Mexico to California and the Founding of San Francisco, 1774 to 1776*. San Diego, CA: Union-Tribune Publishing, 1971.

PULASKI COUNTY ASSOCIATION OF ARKANSAS PIONEERS. *Reminiscences of Arkansas Pioneers*. Pulaski County, AK: The Association, 1986.

RASBURY, RUTH GRANDSTAFF. *The Broad Land: The Life and Times of Stephen Fuller Austin*. Philadelphia: Dorrance, 1972.

RAUSCH, DAVID A., and BLAIR SCHLEPP. *Native American Voices*. Grand Rapids, MI: Baker Books, 1994.

RENNERT, VINCENT PAUL. *Western Outlaws*. New York: Crowell-Collier Press, 1968.

RICE, JULIAN. *Lakota Storytelling: Black Elk, Ella Deloria, and Frank Fools Crow*. New York: P. Lang, 1989.

ROSSI, PAUL A. *The Art of the Old West*. New York: Knopf, 1971.

RUTLEDGE, DON, and RITA ROBINSON. *Center of the World: Native American Spirituality*. North Hollywood, CA: Newcastle, 1992.

SANDERLIN, GEORGE WILLIAM. *The Settlement of California*. New York: Coward, McCann & Geoghegan, 1972.

SANDO, JOE S. *Pueblo Nations: Eight Centuries of Pueblo Indian History*. Santa Fe, NM: Clear Light, 1992.

SAUNDERS, RICHARD. *Ambrose Bierce: The Making of a Misanthrope*. San Francisco: Chronicle Books, 1984.

SAVAGE, WILLIAM SHERMAN. *Blacks in the West*. Westport, CT: Greenwood Press, 1976.

SCHWARZ, MELISSA. *Geronimo: Apache Warrior*. New York: Chelsea House Publishers, 1992.

ST. GEORGE, JUDITH. *The Mount Rushmore Story*. New York: Putnam, 1985.

STOCKEN, H.W. GIBBON. *Among the Blackfoot and Sarcee*. Calgary: Glenbow Museum, 1976.

TAYLOR, ROBERT LEWIS. *A Roaring in the Wind*. New York: Putnam, 1978.

TIME-LIFE BOOKS, ed. *The Indians*. New York: Time-Life Books, 1973.

TRAFZER, CLIFFORD E., ed. *Earth Song / Sky Spirit*. New York: Doubleday, 1993.

TRIMBLE, STEPHEN. *The People: Indians of the American Southwest*. Santa Fe, NM: School of American Research Press, 1993.

TUSKA, JON. *Billy the Kid: His Life and Legend*. Westport, CN: Greenwood Press, 1994.

VOGEL, VIRGIL J. *This Country Was Ours: A Documentary History of the American Indian*. New York: Harper & Row, 1972.

WATTS, PETER CHRISTOPHER. *A Dictionary of the Old West: 1850–1900*. New York: Knopf, 1977.

WELCH, JAMES. *Killing Custer*. New York: Norton, 1994.

WELLMAN, PAUL I. *A Dynasty of Western Outlaws*. New York: Bonanza Books, 1961.

WHEELER, KEITH. *The Old West: The Alaskans*. Alexandria, VA: Time-Life Books, 1977.

WISSLER, CLARK. *Indians of the United States*. Garden City, NY: Doubleday, 1966.

World Book Encyclopedia, The. Chicago: Field Enterprises Educational Corporation, 1976.

MAPS

NATIVE AMERICANS

LAND ACQUIRED BY THE UNITED STATES

Original Thirteen States

Acquired during the Revolution and by treaty of 1783

Florida Purchase 1819

Louisiana Purchase from France 1803

Texas Annexation 1845

Gadsden Purchase 1853

Oregon County by treaty with Great Britain 1846

Mexican Cession of 1848

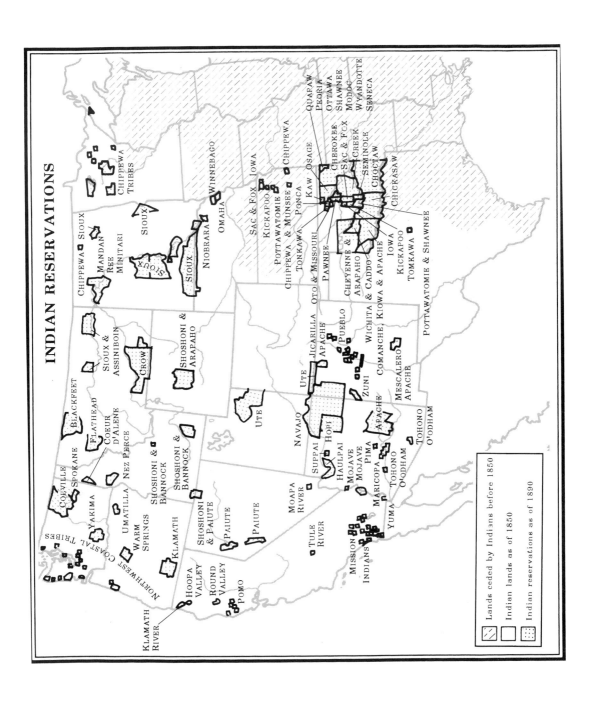

INDIAN RESERVATIONS

Lands ceded by Indians before 1850

Indian lands as of 1850

Indian reservations as of 1890

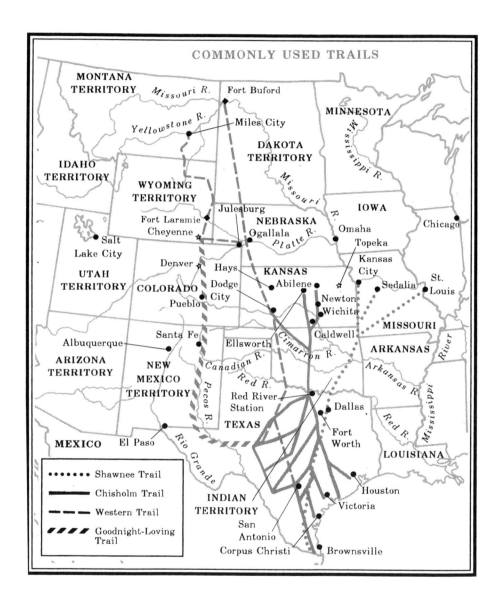

COMMONLY USED TRAILS

- •••••• Shawnee Trail
- —————— Chisholm Trail
- – – – – Western Trail
- ▨▨▨ Goodnight-Loving Trail

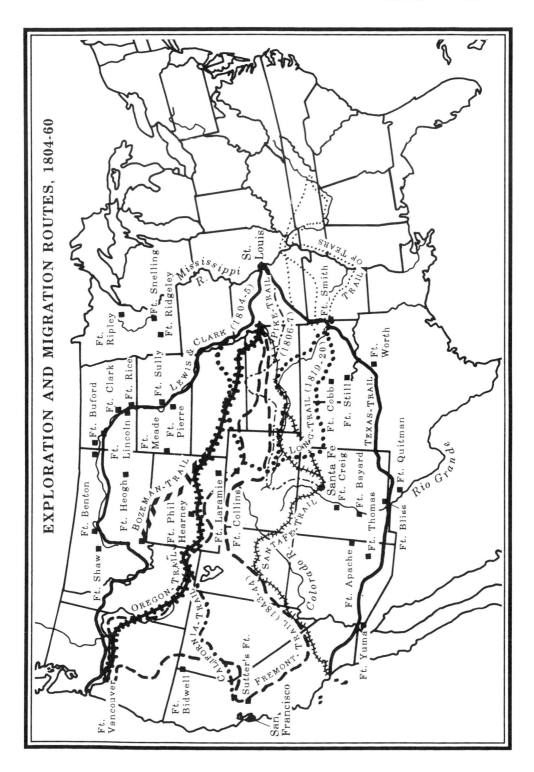

EXPLORATION AND MIGRATION ROUTES, 1804-60

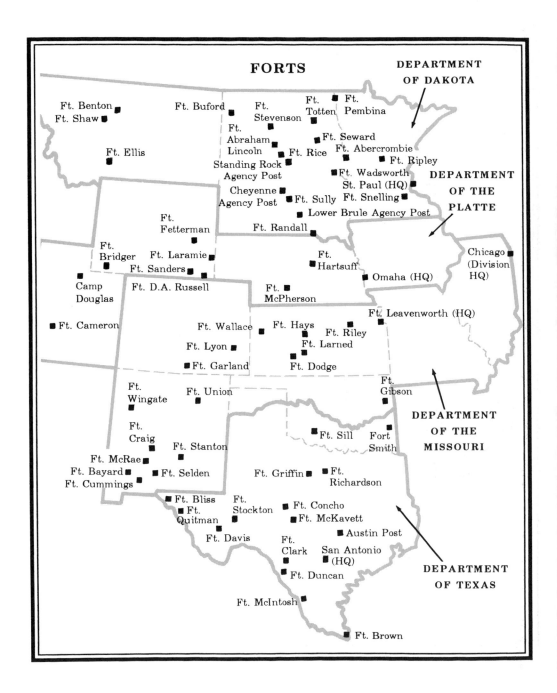

FORTS

DEPARTMENT
OF DAKOTA

Ft. Benton
Ft. Shaw

Ft. Buford

Ft.
Stevenson

Ft.
Totten

Ft.
Pembina

Ft. Ellis

Ft.
Abraham
Lincoln

Ft. Rice

Ft. Seward

Ft. Abercrombie

Ft. Ripley

Standing Rock
Agency Post

Ft. Wadsworth

St. Paul (HQ)

DEPARTMENT
OF THE
PLATTE

Cheyenne
Agency Post

Ft. Sully

Ft. Snelling

Lower Brule Agency Post

Ft.
Fetterman

Ft. Randall

Ft.
Hartsuff

Ft.
Bridger

Ft. Laramie

Ft. Sanders

Omaha (HQ)

Chicago
(Division
HQ)

Camp
Douglas

Ft. D.A. Russell

Ft.
McPherson

Ft. Cameron

Ft. Wallace

Ft. Hays

Ft. Riley

Ft. Leavenworth (HQ)

Ft. Lyon

Ft. Larned

Ft. Garland

Ft. Dodge

Ft.
Gibson

Ft.
Wingate

Ft. Union

DEPARTMENT
OF THE
MISSOURI

Ft.
Craig

Ft. Stanton

Ft. Sill

Fort
Smith

Ft. McRae

Ft. Bayard
Ft. Cummings

Ft. Selden

Ft. Griffin

Ft.
Richardson

Ft. Bliss

Ft.
Quitman

Ft.
Stockton

Ft. Concho

Ft. McKavett

Ft. Davis

Ft.
Clark

San Antonio
(HQ)

Austin Post

DEPARTMENT
OF TEXAS

Ft. Duncan

Ft. McIntosh

Ft. Brown

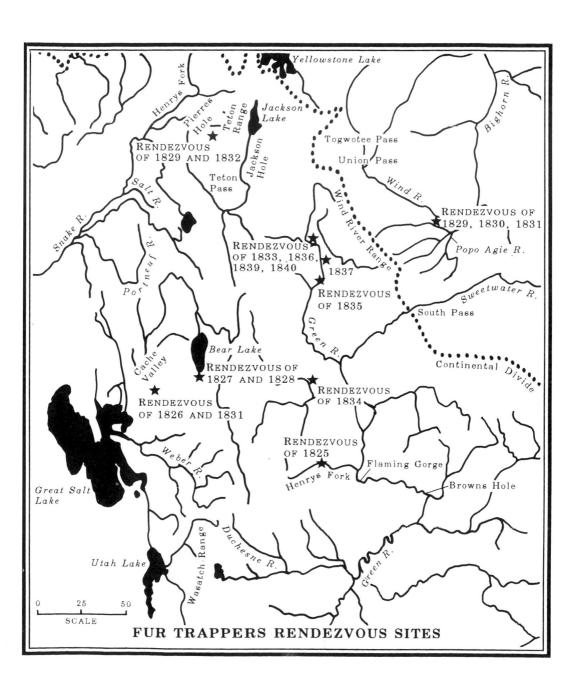

FUR TRAPPERS RENDEZVOUS SITES

PRIMARY WESTERN MINING SITES, 1848-1900

INDEX

ABOUT THE CONTRIBUTORS

Robert M. Utley has served as historian for the Defense Department Joint Chiefs of Staff, as well as chief historian for the National Parks Service. He is the author of a dozen books on Western America history, most recently *The Lance and the Shield: The Life and Times of Sitting Bull* (1993).

Dale L. Walker is a freelance writer and former director of Texas Western Press, at the University of Texas/El Paso. He is a past president of Western Writers of America, and is the author of 13 books, including *Buckey O'Neill: The Story of a Rough Rider* (1985), and over 400 articles on military and Western American history.

Jace Weaver is the author of *Then to the Rock Let Me Fly: Luther Bohanon and Judicial Activism* (1993), as well as numerous articles on Native American issues. He is also an attorney and a Ph.D. candidate in Native American religions at Union Theological Seminary, in New York.

George R. Robinson is an award-winning journalist. His work has appeared in a wide range of publications, including *The New York Times, The Washington Post, New York Newsday, Publishers Weekly,* and *The Progressive.*

Shelley Rossell writes frequently on historical subjects.

Arnie Bernstein is a writer.